The Crown of the Virgin

THE
CROWN
OF THE
VIRGIN

An Ancient Meditation
on Mary's Beauty,
Virtue, and Sanctity

attributed to
St. Ildephonsus of Toledo

translated by
FR. ROBERT NIXON, OSB
Abbey of the Most Holy Trinity
New Norcia, Western Australia

TAN Books
Gastonia, North Carolina

Cover design by Caroline Green

Cover image: *The Madonna of the Magnificat*, detail of the Virgin's face and crown, 1482 (tempera on panel), Botticelli, Sandro (Alessandro di Mariano di Vanni Filipepi), Photo © Raffaello Bencini

ISBN: 978-1-5051-1784-4
Kindle ISBN: 978-1-5051-1785-1
ePUB ISBN: 978-1-5051-1786-8

Published in the United States by
TAN Books
PO Box 269
Gastonia, NC 28053
www.TANBooks.com

Printed in India

Ad Majorem Gloriam Virginis Mariae

Lily of love, pure and inviolate!
Tower of ivory! red rose of fire!
Thou hast come down our darkness to illume:
For we, close-caught in the wide nets of Fate,
Wearied with waiting for the World's Desire,
Aimlessly wandered in the house of gloom,
Aimlessly sought some slumberous anodyne
For wasted lives, for lingering wretchedness,
Till we beheld thy re-arisen shrine,
And the white glory of thy loveliness.

Oscar Wilde, 1879

CONTENTS

TRANSLATOR'S NOTE

The text presented in the following pages is a translation from a Latin work entitled *Libellus de Corona Virginis,* or "The Little Book on the Crown of the Virgin." In it the author imaginatively fashions a crown, decorated with twelve jewels, six stars, and six flowers. Each of these is interpreted as representing particular aspects of the beauty, beneficence, virtue, or sanctity of the Blessed Virgin. The use of the image, suggested by Scripture,[1] of a bejewelled crown as the formal and conceptual basis of devotional writing to our Lady is by no means unique to the present work—innumerable other examples are to be found dating from the end of the Middle Ages through to the early modern era.[2] Yet the present work, apart from consid-

---

[1] Rv 12:1; Ps 21:3; Prv 4:9; Sg 7:5; Sir 45:14.

[2] See Maurice de Villepreux, *Nova Corona Mariae* (Paris: Johannes Argentoracensis, 1512), Pelbartus de Temesvár, *Stellarium Coronae Gloriossimae Virginis* (Venice: Jo. Ant. Bertanus, 1586), Isidorus de S. Aegidio, *Corona Stellarum Duodecim* (Antwerp: Henricus van Dunwalt, 1685).

erations of its perhaps considerably greater antiquity, remains distinguished amongst this literary *corpus* of Marian crowns.

According to its earliest editor, "It glories in heart-felt piety, in cordial affection and in mellifluous sweetness to an extent that I have encountered in no other writings of the saints or doctors of the Church; (nor indeed have I found anything which) seizes the soul of the reader more sweetly, or inflames it to devotion to the Virgin more ardently."[3]

Another compiler opines that "we scarcely believe that (this small book) could be read without it inspiring an intimate sense of piety and devotion towards the Mother of God."[4]

The work is found in a single manuscript source only, from which the various published editions (of which mention will be made shortly) all derive, either directly or indirectly. This manuscript is held in the venerable library of the Cathedral of Toledo and is of unknown

---

[3] Pedro de Alba y Astorga, *Bibliotheca Virginalis, sive Mariae Mare Magnum, Tomus II* (Madrid: Typogr. Regia, 1648), 360-61.

[4] L. Vives (ed.), *Liber precum in quo variae et multae egregiae preces ad usum cleri tum regularis tum secularis, Tomus II* (Paris: Bibliopolam, 1857), 387.

date, but apparently "most ancient."[5] While no author is identified in the manuscript, the text is located in a codex containing various writings of St. Ildephonsus, to whom it has therefore appeared reasonable to attribute the authorship.

Ildephonsus (c.607–c.670) was a monk at the monastery of Agali, in the vicinity of the imperial centre of Toledo, where he later served as abbot. He became archbishop of that illustrious city in 659, succeeding his uncle, Eugenius II. According to St. Julian, who succeeded him in his archepiscopal office, Ildephonsus was "rich with the fear of God, devout in religion, profuse in compunction, grave in carriage, praiseworthy in honesty, singular in patience, silent in guarding secrets, and of the highest wisdom. He was brilliant in his ingenuity of speech, and fluent in his eloquence."[6]

A well-known tradition relates that the Virgin Mary herself appeared to Ildephonsus and presented him with a chasuble. This anecdote is related thus by one writer:

> When once (Ildephonsus) was attending a nightly prayer vigil (in honor of the Immaculate

5   de Alba, *Bibliotheca Virginalis,* 361.
6   Julian of Toledo, *Beati HIldefonsi Elogium,* PL 96:43-44.

Conception of the Blessed Virgin), the church seemed suddenly to blaze with radiant light, beyond what any mortal eyes could bear. Everyone else present fell to the ground, struck with terror. But Ildephonsus alone dauntlessly proceeded to the altar, and fell to his knees and prayed fervently. He perceived the Blessed Virgin herself, seated in his own episcopal throne, in aspect more glorious than any mortal being. She spoke to him in these words, "The reward you will receive for defending the honor of my perpetual virginity will be a special gift from the treasury of Heaven!" She then placed upon him a chasuble, saying, "My son, henceforth celebrate all the annual feasts held in my honor vested in this garment."[7]

He was a vigorous champion of the doctrine of the perpetual virginity of Mary, which is the theme of his best-known work, *On the Perpetual Virginity of Most Blessed Mary.*[8]

---

[7] Carl Stengel, *Imagines Sanctorum Ordinis S. Benedicti* (Augsburg: Benediktinerkloster St. Ulrich und Afra, 1652), 16.

[8] Cf. Ildephonsus of Toledo, *De Virginitate perpetua SS. Mariae,* PL 96:53-110.

The attribution of the present work to Ildephonsus is not, it must be noted, unproblematic. There are certain indisputable anachronisms in the text, notably borrowings of phrases from hymns, prayers, or writings, that are of later origin.[9] There are also notable discrepancies in vocabulary between the works of Ildephonsus of which the authorship is more certain.[10] On the other hand certain literary traits which characterize the *Corona*, such as the rhythmic accumulation of long and intentionally repetitive series of titles, invocations, descriptions, and petitions, are prominent characteristics of Ildephonsus's style elsewhere. Given that the work is attributed to no particular author in the manuscript, it seems not impossible that the copyist of the single extant manuscript may have introduced textual variants, additions, or "improvements" in transcribing

---

[9]   An obvious example of this is the appearance of the phrase, "*illos tuos misericordes oculos ad me converte*", clearly borrowed from the *Salve Regina*, in chapter 2.

[10]   For example, in *De Virginitate perpetua SS. Mariae,* Ildephonsus employs the terms "*Dominatrix*" and "*Genitrix.*" (PL 96:58) Yet the *Corona,* despite the otherwise exhaustive multitude of titles it uses for the Blessed Virgin, does not include either word. On the other hand, the *Corona* uses the title "*Domina nostra*" ("Our Lady"), (cf. prologue and chapter 17) which does not feature in any of the other writings of Ildephonsus.

an earlier work. But it could also simply be a later work which emulates some of the literary features and devotional themes of Ildephonsus's writing, with which the scribe who created the manuscript was clearly familiar.

To date, the *Corona* has been presented to the reading public in five editions. The most significant are those of Pedro de Alba y Astorga, OFM, dating from 1648,[11] and of Francisco de Lorenzana, Archbishop of Toledo, dating from 1782.[12] Both of these editions derive from (apparently) the same manuscript in the Toledo Cathedral library. Nevertheless, there are a few textual discrepancies (albeit of a minor nature) between the 1648 and the 1782 editions. These, in the main, emerge simply from the correction of the typographical errors and misreadings of the manuscript, which abound in de Alba's earlier edition. The text of the 1782 edition, certainly the more reliable of the two, was reproduced in three nineteenth-century compilations: a *Liber Precum*

---

[11]   Ildephonsus of Toledo (attrib.), "Libellus de Corona Virginis," in Pedro de Alba y Astorga, *Bibliotheca Virginalis, II* (Madrid: Typographia Regia, 1648), 362-83.

[12]   Ildephonsus of Toledo (attrib.), "Libellus de Corona Virginis," in Francisco de Lorenzana, *SS. PP. Toletanorum quotquot extant Opera, Tomus I* (Toledo: Ioachimum Ibarra, 1782), 394-434.

edited by Louis Vives,[13] the *Summa aurea de laudibus Beatissimae Virginis Mariae* edited by J. P. Migne,[14] and the ubiquitous *Patrologia Latina* of the same editor.[15]

As in any translation, the rendering given here is necessarily a compromise between fidelity to the original and the demands of idiomatic English. Latin is, of course, rich in words which are more-or-less but not-quite synonymous (e.g., *pulchra, speciosa, decora, formosa*, etc. for "beautiful"), for which precise or acceptable English equivalents do not always spring readily to hand, especially when several (or, indeed, many) such words are used in immediate succession. The translator has been guided in such instances not only by the primary question of replicating the meaning intended by the author but also by considerations of idiom, sonority, rhythm, and readability.

---

13   Ildephonsus of Toledo (attrib.), "Libellus de Corona Virginis," in L. Vives (ed.), *Liber precum, II*, 387-458.

14   Ildephonsus of Toledo (attrib.), "Libellus de Corona Virginis," in J.P. Migne (ed.), *Summa aurea de laudibus Beatissimae Virginis Mariae, Tomus XIII* (Paris: Migne, 1862), 1247-75.

15   Ildephonsus of Toledo (attrib.), "Libellus de Corona Virginis," in J.P. Migne (ed.), *Patrologia Latina, Tomus XCVI* (Paris: Migne, 1862), 283-318.

In translating the names of gemstones and stars, English terms which are in current general usage have been favored as far as possible. For example, *carbunculus* has been translated as "ruby" rather than the punctiliously literal option of "carbuncle" (a now somewhat dated term) or the more mineralogically accurate "almandine garnet." For similar reasons, *chrysoprasus* has been given as "jade" rather than the more literal "chrysoprase."

In those passages presented in verse, a higher degree of translational, or indeed paraphrastic, liberty has been freely exercised, wherever it seems more faithfully or more felicitously to convey the spirit and qualities of the original text.

It is the sincere hope and prayer of the present translator—just as it was of the original author—that this work may serve to promote love of and devotion to the glorious and Blessed Virgin Mary, who remains, now as always, our life, our sweetness, and our hope.

Fr. Robert Nixon, OSB
Abbey of the Most Holy Trinity
New Norcia, Western Australia

PROLOGUE

by the Author

"There shall be a crown of gold upon her head, as a visible sign of her sanctity."

Ecclesiasticus 45:14

Sacred Scripture teaches us, all creation urges us, mystical symbols warn us, and every page of holy theology instructs us that we should never cease to bless, to praise, and to proclaim the imperial majesty of the most glorious Virgin Mary. For she is decorated with the glory of every imaginable virtue, adorned with finest pearls of all heavenly gifts, and rendered splendid by the radiance of divine wisdom and knowledge. We are warmly called to her praise by wonderful miracles, by oracles descending from heaven itself, through hidden mysteries, through the teaching of the prophets, through mystical signs, through the words of the Holy

Gospel, and through the clarion call of the Lord's holy apostles.

The most exalted heavens praise her, together with the sun and the moon, the stars of the firmament, the whole orb of the earth, the choirs and legions of holy angels, and all the host of celestial spirits. For this reason, holy people and saints of every nation under heaven, inspired by the Holy Spirit, have always endeavored to extol her with wondrous praise, with golden eloquence, and with mellifluous and noble speech. I myself, who have by no means been so copiously or egregiously endowed with any such talents, will, nevertheless, elucidate and show forth her praise as far as my own small abilities permit. I, who am indeed a mere stammering rustic, do this only by virtue of the grace mercifully given me. Indeed, were I not to do so, I could rightly be judged to have failed in my duty of gratitude for the fruitful blessings Mother Mary has shown me.

In order that—in accordance with the verse of Scripture quoted above[16]—our Lady's most revered head may shine forth with fitting splendor, I shall fashion for her a golden crown, adorned with twelve precious gems, made radiant with six stars of celestial light, and

---

[16]   Sirach 45:14.

perfumed with six of the most beautiful flowers so that it may indeed be filled with all imaginable sweetness!

In the following chapters, these shall be described in the order of their placement in this crown. And I shall position them thus:

- in the first place, a precious topaz;
- in the second place, the morning-star, Sirius;
- in the third place, a carnelian stone;
- in the fourth place, a lily;
- in the fifth place, a chalcedony;
- in the sixth place, the star Arcturus;
- in the seventh place, a sapphire;
- in the eighth place, a crocus flower;
- in the ninth place, an agate stone;
- in the tenth place, the Star of the Sea;
- in the eleventh place, a jasper;
- in the twelfth place, a rose;
- in the thirteenth place, a ruby;
- in the fourteenth place, the Sun;
- in the fifteenth place, an emerald;
- in the sixteenth place, a violet;
- in the seventeenth place, an amethyst;
- in the eighteenth place, the Moon;

- in the nineteenth place, a peridot gemstone;
- in the twentieth place, a sunflower;
- in the twenty-first place, a stone of precious gold-green jade;
- in the twenty-second place, the star Orion;
- in the twenty-third place, a beryl; and, finally,
- in the twenty-fourth place, a daisy flower.

May such an array of precious jewels, of glowing stars, of beautiful flowers, render the crown which I shall fashion more noble, more beautiful, and more pleasing to our gracious Lady!

Therefore, I beg you, O Virgin most pure and merciful, most noble and radiant Queen, to accept benignly this humble token of my service. By your grace, may you receive me into your protection and guard me from all the perils which surround me. Let my voice be joined—I earnestly entreat you—with the glorious choirs of heavenly angels who sing your praises!

And may you generously show, O great Virgin Queen, your peaceful and serene countenance to all your sons and daughters of grace who glorify you and who beg for your unfailing help. By your intercession, may we merit mercy for our sins. And by your guidance and example, may we come at last to the glory of paradise! Amen.

CHAPTER I

ON WHY A CROWN IS FITTING FOR OUR LADY

In the longing of my soul, in the joy of the Holy Spirit, in the most genuine love, and in the Word of Truth, I wish to extol you, to praise you, and to bless you, O Virgin Mary! For you are more radiant than the Sun; in appearance, you are more beautiful; in faith and grace, you are richer. Indeed, you are the most beautiful of all created beings; and serene, radiant, and pleasing, as lovable as the fragrant rose, wholly entrancing and utterly attractive. Such is your dignity and excellence, that were I in possession of the tongues of humans and of angels, and understood all hidden mysteries, and had all the knowledge of Scripture, these resources should fail me long before I had succeeded in expressing even the beginnings of the praise due to you. For you indeed are incomparably above all women in beauty, in gracefulness, and in elegance. You surpass all mortals in virtue, grace, and wisdom. You are more glorious than the angels themselves in eminence of dignity, in excellence of holiness, and in command of glory and honor. Exalted above the choirs of angels, above the thrones of the apostles and the prophets, and above all heavenly beings, you sit—crowned as Queen, at the right hand of your most beloved Son!

There your merits are proclaimed, your honor gloriously extolled, and your praises and privileges sung forth by all, with the deepest veneration and most fervent devotion.

What, therefore, am I, a miserable sinner, able to add to such ineffable splendor, to such transcendent glory? But may my humble pen strive for this goal alone—that it may contribute the merest drop, however small, to the limitless ocean of your immortal praise . . .

The crown which I would fashion for you, O Mistress, fittingly ought to be fashioned of purest gold. For just as gold excels all other metals in value and rarity so you have primacy above all others, both in heaven and on earth. To you every knee shall bend, in heaven and on earth and in the underworld; and every tongue shall proclaim you to be the unique and honored Mother of our Lord Jesus Christ, in the glory of God the Father.

Within the celestial reality of eternity, you are clothed with the sun as in a robe and crowned with the interwoven radiance of twelve dazzling stars, and adorned with all conceivable glory and splendor. Just as gold is outstanding for its brilliance and beauty, so you, O beloved Queen, are most bright in your sanctity, most refulgent in your virtues and miracles, most radiant in your outstanding merits, and most indescribably lovely and attractive in both your mind and body.

Prayer

O Virgin Queen, clothed with the Sun, crowned with twelve stars, and raised up to the highest heavens, you are most merciful! You are more radiant than the Star of the Sea!

Behold the hostile spears by which I am pierced. See the bitter sorrows by which I am tormented. Look upon the grave temptations by which I am tested. Lest the enemy should continue to attack me, lest he should overturn and overcome me, may your right hand cast him down into hell from whence he came. And lest the light of faith should ever grow dark to me, may the ray of your splendor shine always upon me.

For as long as grim death may threaten our bodies, and past ills may trouble our minds, and our consciences stand burdened by sin and trembling with guilt, may your gracious presence continue to assist us kindly.

Defend us by your gentle protection, that we be not disturbed or overcome by our foes. And may we pass—secure in the hope of the holy resurrection—to the glory of eternal light. Amen.

CHAPTER 2

THE PRECIOUS TOPAZ,

in the First Place in the Crown of the Virgin

O Virgin, full of every grace, wholly radiant and serene! You are the sacred and blessed resting place for the Son of God, resplendent in gold and dazzling in loveliness and glory! In the first place in your magnificent crown I shall place a topaz, excelling the sparkle of all other stones. This I do hoping to reflect the praise and glory of your singular excellence. This topaz is well suited to be an ornament of your crown, O most sweet Mistress; for just as you excel all women in the beauty of your flesh, so also you surpass all saints and angels in the excellence of your holiness. For your whole life stands as an example of sanctity and perfection, and a model of the most impeccable purity of morals.

If one considers faith, who was ever richer
in it than you?
If one considers hope,
who was ever more patient or more
unwavering?
If love, who was more fervent?
Who was ever more studious in sacred
reading?
Or more devout in prayer?
Or more subtle in contemplation?
Or more sincere in piety?
Or more clement in mercy?
Or purer in chastity?
Or more spotless in virginity and
temperance?
Or more generously endowed with divine
knowledge?
Or more eloquent in justice?
Or stronger in the face of adversity?

What angel or saint ever penetrated more deeply
into the heavenly mysteries?
Who ever drew divine grace more fully into themselves than you?

Or who ever perceived with more clarity and illumination the ineffable majesty of the Most High God?

Therefore, O Mistress, you shall deservedly have as an ornament of your head this topaz—a jewel more stunning than all other stones! For you surpass all other saints and angels in beauty of virtue, in splendor of holy charisms, and in the merits by which you are crowned. Because of the loveliness of all the good qualities you possess and the generous fruitfulness of all your mercies, you draw sinners to reconciliation. You encourage all those who struggle to fight on to the crown of their victorious reward, and you lead the just to the prize of eternal glory.

O Empress of the earth, and Queen of Heaven, when you bore your glorious Son—who was also the Son of God and our Savior—you abolished our servitude and restored our liberty! You conquered death and granted us new life. You refresh us in our anxiety; you comfort us in our adversity; you strengthen us in our weakness; you liberate us from the domain of death; you rescue us from demons; you save us from eternal damnation; you open the gates of paradise to us; you unite us with our precious Redeemer!

O Mother of mercy, you untie that which is bound up; you lighten our afflictions; you heal the wounded;

you obtain mercy for sinners; you revive those who are failing; you restore those who have fallen away; you give hope to those who despair. You renew honor; you rejuvenate faith; you pour forth grace and new strength. You alleviate anger; you restore our lost inheritance; you separate us from the devil; you purify us from sin—O most gracious Mother, you reconcile us to God himself!

Prayer

O Virgin of aureate radiance, most holy Mother of God, joy of the angels, exaltation of the patriarchs, happiness of the prophets, felicity of the apostles, sweetness of the martyrs, nectar of those who profess the Truth, harmony of the holy virgins!

> Turn, in kindness, your benign ear towards
> me,
> let your eyes of mercy gaze upon me.
> I am blind; grant me light!
> I am weak; give me strength!
> I am dead; make me live!

By the honeyed vision of your beauty, the sorrowful are made joyful. By your gentle touch, the infirm are made whole. By your rose-like odour, the dead are raised to life. All the good things which come from heaven are given through your merits, or obtained through your kindly intercession.

O Mistress, look, therefore, upon me—a wretched sinner, darkened by iniquity, surrounded by a multitude of miseries! Through you, most holy Virgin, let my chains be broken, let my sins be forgiven, let what is broken within me be repaired, let what has grown weary be renewed, let what is lost be found, let what is incomplete be rendered whole. Through your grace, let my will be cleansed, let my mind be clarified, my soul inflamed, my heart melt, my taste be filled with sweetness, my appearance be made as beautiful as God intended.

Come to my aid—O you who are the light by which I am illuminated, the sweetness by which I am refreshed, the strength by which I become strong, and the fortitude by which I am sustained. Cast far away from me the false and wicked word, the malevolent thought, and the evil deed. May your grace direct my life; may your presence enlighten my mind; and may your mercy lead me unto life eternal.

For you are, indeed, the true and surest path to that glory!

O Mother! Through you the way is illuminated which leads to the heights of heaven, where, through your intercession, the assembly of the humble will be graciously received.

O Thou honey of ineffable sweetness, O Thou glowing brilliance of the spring's flowers!

O Mistress of the Cosmos, O blessed bond of charity, O unique union of love!

You wash away our guilt, you cleanse us of our sin.

You are the supreme maidenly Dignity, decorated with lilies.

You are the unique, fruitful Virginity, enthroned on high.

Queen of the angels, life-giving medicine, mysterious flower of the valley!

Teacher of virtue and light of every heart!

Celestial Queen, protectress of the faithful, ivory throne of Christ, lead us, thy children, to the glory of the saints when this, our earthly exile, is complete. Amen.

CHAPTER 3

THE MORNING-STAR, SIRIUS,

in the Second Place in the Crown of the Virgin

You, O illustrious Virgin, happy gate of heaven, pleasure of paradise, Empress of the angels, Queen of the world, joy of the saints, advocate of the faithful, fortitude of those who struggle, gentle shepherdess of those who have wandered astray, healing balm of the penitent—to the praise and glory of your imperial majesty, in the second place in your most glorious crown, I shall place the star Sirius—the morning star, the brightest light of the celestial firmament. This sidereal body is of a spherical form. It is clear and lucid, beautiful and gracious.

And each of these qualities befit you perfectly, most holy Lady—and hence it is only right that this star be placed in your crown. Eternity is designated in its circular and round form, having neither beginning nor end. And while you had a beginning in the realm of time, in the sight of God you truly existed eternally. From the beginning, before the commencement of time, you were foreknown and predestined eternally in the presence of the divine majesty. You were chosen before the creation of the world as the Mother of God, holy and immaculate—that through you alone, God would send his peace to us from the heavens, and would redeem the human race, repair the ruins of the angelic host, lead to freedom those enchained in the dark dungeons of hell, and unlock the gates of heaven itself! You were indeed radiant in your holy acts, yet even more radiant in your saving example, and most superlatively radiant of all in your glorious merits!

In the sight of God, you were lovable and pleasing, gracious beyond the beauty of all other women, elegant beyond the splendor of angels. How great are your merits, O Mother of God! How immense the sweetness of your mercy and piety! You restore what is earthly, you repair what is heavenly, you join the lowest to the highest, and you mercifully bestow grace upon all those who cry out to you. Therefore, whoever is in need of forgiveness may confidently flee to you and will find your heart to overflow with abundant mercy.

And whoever, out of some troubled impulse, finds themselves doubting their Faith—they need only look to you, and they will be solidly confirmed in right belief. Whoever is tempted by some urge of the flesh may confidently invoke your grace, and the peril to their chastity will be promptly taken away. Whoever is struck in their heart by foolish pride or elation need only turn their glance to you, and the proud swelling of their soul will be reduced by the merits of your humility. Whoever finds themself set ablaze by the fire of wrath may raise their eyes to you and will become meek by virtue of your own perfect tranquillity. Whoever is led by some error away from the path of true life may gaze at you, as at the Star of the Sea, and they will be led back to the way of truth by means of your most gracious light.

In all perils your mercy helps us and is indeed the most powerful help of all to us. And this is but fitting, since you are nothing less than the Mother of God, Queen of the world, Empress of the heavens, and beloved spouse of the Holy Spirit! You help us to remain in Christ and to ascend to divine things. In the eternity of God, you flower miraculously. In the truth of God, you shine splendidly. In the goodness of God, you rejoice exultingly. You return to grace those who have been separated from it by sin, you reconcile them to holiness, you put guilt to flight, and you wash away all vices. You return innocence to the fallen and joy to those who know sorrow. You drive away hatred and you bestow peace. Wars you settle, wrath you disarm, the proud you make humble, and the humble you ardently love. You reconcile the earthly to the heavenly, and that which is most lowly to that which is most highly exalted.

Indeed, you gave birth to the God of heaven, the King of the earth, the Lord of the universe, the Healer of the world, the Destroyer of death, the Restorer of life, the Author of eternity. In conceiving him you felt no sinful lust, and in bearing him you felt no pain. For the blessed birth of our Savior, I offer this jubilant hymn of praise!

> O Beloved Creator of the stars,
> Born before the dawn's primordial light,
> Inspired by a desire to save this fallen world,
> Into the melancholy twilight of its dark-
> ened ruins,

You entered the womb of a radiant maiden,
Like a spouse, lovingly entering his bridal
chamber.

Through the prophets it was foretold,
Through mystical symbols it was
foreshadowed—
This immense, ineffable mystery.
Through the heaven-sent oracle of Gabriel
A clear presentiment was given
To the most gentle Virgin Mary, the chosen
bride of God.

Just as an enthralling scent wafts sweetly
From the flower and the lily,
So from the womb of Mary
The holy Word of the Father is sent forth to
save the world.

Behold the glory of fruitfulness,
And the honor of unstained virginity
United in the graceful body of the Virgin
Mother!
This miraculous glory is as the vitreous
brilliance

Which remains in the richly-hued crimson
    of the rose,
And as the tint and clarity of whiteness
    abides,
Unseen yet radiant, in sable ebony's obsid-
    ian glow.

Since—after God himself—you are the cause of all goodness, I love you and desire to praise you, to adore your beauty, to venerate your beatitude, to glorify your exaltation—and to implore the humble favor of your loving kindness.

PRAYER

O Mother of God, pour out from heaven the light of your mercy so that my soul—which is stained with sin—may be made pure once more by your grace, may be illumined by your glory, may be sweetened by your sweetness, may be inflamed by your love, and may be kept safe by your protection.

May your virginal and divine bearing of the Savior redeem me whom am a captive, heal me who am sick, illuminate me who am blind, grant life to me who am dead, and preserve me from all manner of sin and peril. You alone are my Mistress, whom I shall honor; my sweetness, whom I shall love; my Queen, whom I shall revere; my spouse, whom I shall serve.

Turn the grace of your countenance upon me so that in your beauty I may see light; and in the midst of darkness I may perceive truth; and in the midst of mortal vanity I may see eternal life; and may escape from the black clutches of death.

You are most full of every grace. Therefore cleanse my soul from all malice. Fashion my heart into a temple for God. Fill it with your holy love—so that by loving you, I may desire you; and by desiring you, I may seek you; by seeking you, I may find you; and by finding you, I may embrace you.

And then, O Virgin Queen, I shall hold you forever, and in you alone shall my heart know the sweet solace of heavenly rest. Amen.

CHAPTER 4

THE CARNELIAN GEMSTONE

in the Third Place in the Crown of the Virgin

O Virgin Mother of piety, throne of the divine majesty, all human and angelic natures serve you, and all creation praises you with one exultant voice! At your command, the dry land becomes fertile—that which has grown cold becomes warm, that which is dead springs up with new life. Nothing was ever holier than your saintly life, nothing purer than your immaculate conscience, nothing more blessed than your divine kiss. And nothing is purer than your love, nothing more chaste than your embrace, nothing more beneficial than your aid.

Therefore I—a sinner—gaze upon you lovingly. I yearn longingly but to please you and to pay you my humble homage. And that your crown may be the more richly illustrious, in the third place I insert a stone of precious carnelian, beautiful with the warm luminescence of its violet hue. May this carnelian illumine your noble crown with its deep rubicund glow, even as the spiritual martyrdoms which you sustained, O beloved Mistress, tinctured your soul with glorious crimson and imbued your heart with regal purple.

For you, Mary most holy, sharing in your divine Son's agony, were crushed by unspeakable sorrows, excruciated with untold pains, and tortured with waves of bitterness beyond human comprehension. You beheld your most beloved Son—the adored spouse of your sacred virginity—fallen beneath cruel scourges, spat upon, dishonored and disgraced by human mockery! You beheld him nailed to the bloody gibbet of the cross, forced to drink the bitter chalice of gall and of vinegar, his side torn open with a lance. *You* were also thereby wounded in your gentle mind and pierced in your most noble soul. *You* were also speared through your most tender heart and made a martyr by the black sword of sorrow.

But now rejoice, my Lady—because the One whom you saw die on earth, you now gaze upon reigning as King in heaven! He shall make you—who shared fully his pain—to share also completely in his glory and joy, giving you everlasting and infinite honor. And so every knee shall bend before you, and every tongue shall lovingly proclaim your praise, as Mother of the most high God, spouse of the Holy Spirit, and most beloved daughter of the heavenly Father. You sit at the right hand of the eternal King, as a brilliant Queen, crowned with glory and honor, robed in golden raiment of spell-binding splendor, and lauded unceasingly by the wondrous harmony of choirs of angels and saints!

On account of both the pain of witnessing the death of your Son and the ineffable joy with which you now rejoice in heaven, I wish to salute you in these words:

> Hail, O Virgin most pure,
> Chaste as the snow-white lily,
> You who were pierced by the bitter blade
>   of the cross,
> And transfixed by its savage sword.
> But with the Resurrection of your Son
> You are now joyously exhilarated.
> Your pain is ever put to flight,

And your joy soars to the transcendent
heights.
And now, raised up to the heavens,
You sit, as Queen, gorgeously enthroned:
Enrobed with the sun,
Crowned by the stars,
Applauded with the noble dance
Of the celestial choir of holy virgins;
Forever praised,
Forever acclaimed,
Ceaselessly hailed
By the jubilation of a Cosmos redeemed!
Amen.

It is truly right and just, O most merciful Mistress, that you are glorified and extolled by all creation since you bestow grace feely upon us all and you carry punishments to none. Indeed you grant peace to the earth, grace to the heavens, salvation to the lost, and life to the dead. You bestow what is prosperous and you repel what is perilous. You extinguish vices and enflame virtues. You make the body chaste. You render the heart pure. You grant peace to the body and quiet faith to the mind. You bestow order of life to all peoples and moral goodness to the faithful soul.

For it was you who manifested the Savior to the world in visible form—you bore to the world its holy Redeemer, you gifted to the world its very Creator and Lord. You were foretold by divine heralds and angels, remaining eternally holy in mind and body, exalted by a multitude of singular graces, honored amongst the seraphic princes of the heavenly court, taught and instructed by the Holy Spirit and the wisdom, indeed, of the entire Godhead. You were overshadowed by the virtue of the Most High. You were given the honor of conceiving the immortal Son of God, by the fecund dewfall of the most holy and most mysterious Paraclete.

You are the exemplar of continence and of chastity and the form of perfect integrity. You excel all other created beings, shining high above the darkness of this temporal universe. O holy and devout Virgin, unique in purity! You conceived with inviolate modesty and gave birth to your Son without pains!

And, in doing so, you bore the One who is the true light and life of humanity. You conceived God himself by virtue of his own Holy Spirit, and you bore him without stain. O Virgin beautiful beyond all the daughters of Eve! You conceived in your most chaste womb the One who was beautiful beyond all the sons of Adam. And you gave him unto us—as our Savior and King.

PRAYER

O most clement, most sweet, and most patient Mother of God, have mercy on me at this time—which is my day of tribulation and my time of need. Behold my enemies, how many they are, and how they hate me with a most wicked hate, and how maliciously they persecute me! They would corrupt my soul, they would wound my heart, they would trample me underfoot, like the very dust of the earth.

O my Mistress, reconcile me to my Creator, whom you clothed in your sacred flesh. Return me to my God, whom you nursed upon your virginal bosom.

Enriched by your holy grace, saved by your mercy, illuminated by your light and strengthened by your virtue, may I learn to rise above my enemies, to complete all works of virtue, and to be unfailingly faithful to my Creator.

May I sing unending praises for all eternity—both to him and to you! Amen.

CHAPTER 5

THE RADIANT LILY FLOWER,

in the Fourth Place in the Crown of the Virgin

You, O blessed Mary, are:
the treasury and Edenic garden of blessing,
the column and foundation of true faith,
the splendor and brilliance of grace,
the vessel of mercy and forgiveness,
the Empress of glory, and teacher of Truth,
the foundation of God's Church,
the font of wisdom,
the palace of modesty,
the hope of mercy and of salvation,
the promised land of beatitude,

the Mother of the One who is the Truth
    Itself,
the Mistress of salvation,
the lover of the humble,
the honor of the chaste,
the light of sinners,
the virtue of the penitent,
the instructress of the perfect,
the joy of mortals and of angels.

To add to the glory and beauty of your crown, I will position in the fourth place a lily, a flower both delightful and beautiful. The lily has shining whiteness in its color. It has sweetness in its fragrance, smoothness in its surface, and radiance in its beauty. These attributes are all indeed most apt for your heavenly crown. For in the whiteness of the lily, virginity is signified—and you were the Virgin most pure in heart and most chaste in body. And just as you possessed untainted chastity in your body, so you rejoiced always in perfect innocence and purity in your holy and serene conscience. You were indeed a virgin in giving birth, and you remained forever so—perpetually inviolate, eternally pure. Adorned with the luminescent, roseate glow of maidenhood in your flesh, and in the splendor of purity in your noble soul, you were most pleasing, most beloved, to God the Son—with this, your double ornament of virtue.

You are uniquely our Mistress, our Queen, our teacher. There is none other who pleased God so much, nor built for him so incomparable and so splendid a palace of grace and beauty! And so, just as in comparison to God, none are to be found truly good; so, in comparison to you, none are to be found perfect, none to be found holy.

And what is there which so sweetly enthrals and enraptures the soul as your divine name? Of this holy name, a poet has dared to sing:

> The fragrant name of Mary,
> Showered in golden grace,
> And bewilderingly aromatic—
> An alluring scent
> of the promise of heaven itself!
> It is a light more radiant than the sun.
> It is life—and more than life!—to those
> who lay dead.
>
> And to the humble, silent, and dark-robed
> monk
> It is a sweet and delicious honey,
> Mellifluous nectar from a hallowed source,

Holy, and more than holy—
It is ecstatic and life-giving inebriation;
It is, indeed, nothing less than divine!

You are indeed the Lady most gentle and humble. Sacred Scripture proclaims you to be the Mistress of gentleness, the model of kindness, the rule of modesty and the perfect example of mercy. In truth, you are "the marvellously beautiful maiden, the most lovely of virgins, and wholly unknown by man."[17] There is no other to rival you in beauty, nor in wisdom. And because you are the most captivating of all creatures—with the ornament of purest virginity, the beauty of immaculate sanctity, and the adornment of every possible virtue— you are most pleasing in the eyes of the High King of heaven!

Who could ever suffice to describe your virtues, or to explain your wonders? You are higher than the celestial heavens, and yet more profound than the hidden depths of the ocean. You carried within your womb God himself, whom the entire universe could not contain. You restored that which was lost by our first mother, Eve. And you brought salvation to the human race when we languished, lost in sin, by a singular transaction of

---

[17]   Gn 24:16.

grace and love. You transcend all other creatures and have established a bond between the heavenly and earthly realities, dissolving the chains of sin and death which bound us.

O royal Virgin, ornate with all virtue, you totally captivated the gaze of the angelic citizens of heaven and utterly captured the heart of the King himself! And thus you conceived without sin, and carried your Child without burden, and brought forth God himself to our world. You were the Mother of him whose Father was the Divinity.

You are the flower of flowers, the beloved of the Lord! You are above all virtue and all beauty. Without a touch of shame you were found to be mother of the Savior. You merited to carry the Lord of all, and you alone—O Virgin—were found worthy to nurse the High King of the angels; to illuminate the world with the radiance of your virtues, and to enlighten all faithful hearts with the luminescence of true justice. I salute and hail you, therefore—O Queen of Virgins, fragrant rose of the vernal springtide, purest lily of the valley! And thus saluting you, let me conclude this chapter.

PRAYER

Hail, O you who are full of celestial grace,
And full of God, and full of glory.
The lilies of the holy virgins surround you,
All virtues are your companions,
O Virgin of God, O Virgin Mother,
Who were most gently shaded by the super-
    nal Spirit.
A glowing cloud that illumines the star-be-
    jewelled firmament,
A tower of gleaming ebony,
A noble, crimson-hued rose,
You trample underfoot the gall-drenched
    legions of the Inferno,
And the sword of Divine victory is com-
    mended to you,
As its high and eternal guardian.
You are the healing of humanity,
The Mother of God, the crown of virgins!
Unto you—after God himself—
is the highest honor, glory and praise
Ceaselessly and fittingly due!

Chapter 6

THE PRECIOUS CHALCEDONY STONE,

in the Fifth Place in the Crown of the Virgin

O Lady most miraculous;
  through whom Hades' dark dominions
    were shattered,
  and our Celestial homeland was unlocked;
  Through whom the lost were restored,
  And the wearied elements were made new;
  Aglow with a beauty beyond all,
  Radiant and shining with a singular
    loveliness!

To the honor and glory of your most holy and grace-ful person, in the fifth position in your incomparable crown I place a precious chalcedony stone. This is a stone obscure and dull in the darkness of its native soil, but when it is exposed to the divine light of the sun, it shines most brightly. In your golden diadem, O Mary, it now radiates with the intensity of lightning, illuminating the entire world with your miraculous virtues! For everywhere your name is reverently proclaimed, the holy fruit of your womb is worshipped, and your immaculate heart is profoundly venerated! In every land goes forth the music of your virtues, and the voice of your wonders is heard to the ends of the earth. Throughout the whole globe you enlighten souls, heal bodies, raise up the dead, strengthen the weak, sustain the poor, and bind up broken hearts. You restore sight to the blind, strength to the lame, hearing to the deaf. By your grace, speech is poured forth to the mute, knowledge to the ignorant, and medicine to the sick. By your piety in the sight of God, assistance and mercy is bestowed upon all the afflicted!

O blessed Virgin, and more than blessed! You bore the most blessed of fruit, the holy, immortal Son of God, through whom all things—heaven, and earth, and the seas—partake in divine blessing. At the sight of your beauty, the sun and moon are rendered awestruck. At the slightest motion of your will, the hosts of angels lovingly serve and obey. You are delightful to God, to angels, and to humans: to God, through your humility; to angels, through your purity; and to humans, through your motherhood of our true Savior.

> O vessel filled by perfumes rare,
> With sacred secrets in thy care,
> The exile's true and guiding star,
> And hallowed path to God you are.
>
> The praise of high angelic choirs,
> And balm which perfect health inspires,
> The ark of wisdom's sacred lore,
> And heaven's glowing, radiant door.
>
> Rule of justice, virtue's measure;
> Modest rose, our purest treasure.
> Fruitful olive, guarded bower,
> Garden filled with springtide flowers!
>
> O star of sky and sea,
> We humbly pray to thee,
> From tempest and from woe,
> A harbor safe bestow.

O Queen most radiant, overflowing with all good things! Through you, glory is given to God, joy to the

angels, salvation to sinners, consolation to the despair-
ing, light to the blind, fortitude to those who are strug-
gling, and the glory of an immortal crown to the souls
of the just. You are the medicine healing the sick, the
joy consoling the sorrowful, the balm of those who
know pain.

> You are the most secluded, the most secret
>   of sylvan valleys—
> Cool, shaded, and silent;
> The virgin field neither ploughed nor culti-
>   vated by mortal hand,
> Yet which, divinely fecund,
> Brings forth the highest and most blessed
>   of Fruit:
> Flower of the field, singular lily!
> Christ himself blossomed forth from you.
> You are truly the celestial Elysium,
> The untouched, exalted cedar of the moun-
>   tain never scaled,
> Gently emitting the ethereal vapor of
>   sweetness!

You are the Mother of the Deity, radiant with holy
brightness, and illumining the earth with the clarity of supernal light! As the light of purity itself, you

fashioned a pure dwelling for God himself. In your heavenly throne, you shine above the orders of angels with eternal deifying light, like the dawn star showering the gentle dew of morning upon the meadow. You put to tremulous flight the horrendous and foul darkness which envelops our times, by the dazzling lightning of your virtues. You alone can bring saving medicine to those who now languish in despair. O Mother of our salvation—before whom conquered death trembled, and by whom the lost hope of humanity was restored! You have raised up the ruins of our clouded minds, and restrained the burning fire of our wayward sinfulness.

PRAYER

Have mercy, therefore—O most powerful, most clement, most sweet, most beautiful, most lovely Mary—on me, your humble servant, a contemptible sinner. Cleanse my heart from sin and vice, inflame my soul with your love. Obtain for me from your divine Son forgiveness and peace—and, on the Day of Judgement, a share in his glorious Resurrection! Amen.

CHAPTER 7

THE STAR ARCTURUS,

in the Sixth Place in the Crown of the Virgin

Most serene Queen and inviolate Mother of God—Virgin pure, holy and immaculate—we praise your purity, while we marvel at your humility. But even more lovingly—for it is ever sweeter and more needful to the sinner—we invoke your mercy and clemency. Your perfume is the gift of the Holy Spirit. This Spirit rests in you, illuminating you, and inflaming you with his love. Your Fruit is truly eternal—the fragrance of which fills the world, the taste of which delights the faithful heart, the splendor of which surpasses even the sun in its noontide magnificence!

Because, therefore, as a rich and delicate vine you have borne a Fruit so precious—Jesus Christ, our

Lord—to acknowledge something of your glory and magnificence, in the sixth position in your crown I place the star Arcturus. This star is bright and luminous and decorated with seven lesser stars. These seven lesser stars form around it a constellation in the image of a chariot or wagon. To this form, O Mistress, you may—in a certain way—be compared. For you are star-like in your purity and most dazzling in your faith and sanctity. With seven stars—just as with seven virtues—you are gloriously adorned.

For you were indeed strong through the virtue of *faith*, brightly ablaze through the virtue of *love*, raised to the heights through the virtue of *hope*. Through the virtue of *temperance*, you were sober and modest. Through the virtue of *fortitude*, you were most constant; through the virtue of *justice*, most equitable; and through the virtue of *prudence*, most wise.

And you indeed served as the chariot of God, carrying in your holy soul God Almighty, and holding in your sacred womb our Lord Jesus Christ. You are indeed the chariot of the true Israel; that is, the Church—kindly imploring peace and mercy for our sins and exhibiting the pathway which leads to paradise. My Mistress! Consolation of my heart, sweetness of my soul, refreshment of my spirit! Mercifully correct and amend my stony and beast-like ways. Through your merits, grant to me peace and forgiveness. Through your very self, let the way to paradise be revealed to me and let the doors of heaven be unbolted!

O Lady most illustrious, teach me what I may offer that would be pleasing to you. Demonstrate to me what I may present that would be acceptable, what gift I may give that would be worthy of your beauty and love. Parch the thirst of this contemptible sinner with the fruitful rain of your stainlessness; nourish this horrid worm with the richness of your sweetness. Rescue me from the dark forces which surround me, and confound those who would destroy my soul! May my spiritual enemies be dispersed like smoke and shadows. May they perish, crushed by your power, O great Lady. May the Inferno swallow them alive!

Open—O Key of David!—the depths of your honey-flowing heart. Open the gate of your immortal light, that I may enter and see, and taste the sweetness of your kiss, and that my thirsting soul may be inebriated by your most sweet gaze. Out of this miraculous refreshment, may I learn to love you with my whole heart and mind—fervently and prudently, sincerely and joyously, humbly and devoutly. Grant to me such a voice of exultant praise that I may fittingly proclaim your wonders!

Blessed is your flower-adorned chastity, and blessed is your virginal motherhood! Blessed is your gracious humility, and blessed is your heart-felt piety. Blessed is your unique sanctity by which you are rendered more excellent than all other created beings, and blessed is that special dignity by which you are rendered more precious than the entire created universe!

For the Holy Spirit—as a mellifluous dewfall from on high—made you conceive within your womb. Through a divine overshadowing, the Dove of heaven lovingly shaded your most holy body. The same Spirit indelibly signed your most blessed soul as the noble and unique resting place of the entire Trinity. Thus your spirit was adorned with the gold of faith, the silver of wisdom, the priceless gems of sanctity, the roses of modesty, the lilies of chastity, and the violets of virginity! Thus was your immaculate heart illuminated by the Sun of justice and made radiant by the moon of chastity and the stars of innocence. You were decorated with the ornaments of all graces and made unspeakably noble with the sacred anointing of perfect holiness.

Prayer

O Virgin Lady, elevated and filled by so many and by such graces! May you be merciful to us in our needs, sweet in our tribulations, merciful in our anxieties, and quick to help in our perils. You indeed are the refuge of the troubled, the solace of the sorrowful. You gently wipe away the tears of those who mourn. We—your children—are pressed down by the weight of our sins, flooded by the turbulent waves of vain desire, and battered by the acrid waves of empty pleasures.

But, O, have mercy upon us! Lest we be enwrapped in perpetual darkness and consigned to eternal woe—help us in the hour of sadness and in the hour when fearful death draws nigh. Lead us to the bliss of the holy Resurrection and to the joy of immortal light! Amen.

CHAPTER 8

THE PRECIOUS SAPPHIRE,

in the Seventh Place in the Crown of the Virgin

O noble abode of the Holy Trinity, hallowed resting place of the supernal Word of the Father, beautiful maiden, exquisite Virgin, serene, sweet, and merciful Queen, full of divine grace! You were eternally chosen by God as the first amongst consecrated women. You, by celestial right, merited to imitate the lives of the angels. Into your heart, the heavens poured forth with untold abundance the fullness of grace—like the very dewfall of morn—transforming you into the holy dwelling place of God himself, making you to become the most exalted of all heavenly blessings!

With the great multitude of your miraculous wonders proclaimed everywhere, I—an unworthy sinner but desirous of magnifying further your glory—humbly venture to insert in the seventh place in your crown a most precious sapphire. This sapphire resembles the tranquil skies, which when struck by the rays of the sun, shine forth with a burning, azure luminescence. And this gem is a most fitting adornment to your gracious crown. For you, O gracious Lady, are most splendid and serene, most pure, sincere and delightful. You are the immaculate perfection of beauty and of grace, and the pinnacle of incomparable loveliness!

No stain darkens you, nor does any shadow of a fault cloud you. You are more dazzling and radiant than the sun itself, and outshine the whole firmament of the starry heavens in exquisite radiance. But when that Highest Divine Majesty, whose beloved spouse and cherished daughter you are, illuminates your face with his ray of grace, then you—O my hope—increase yet further in beauty! Your wisdom radiates with a yet more penetrating light. Your perfect love of God burns with a yet more intense ardour. You indeed, gracious Mistress, make chaste the minds and bodies of all who look towards you with love. Your beauteous glance has power to nullify and to expurgate the heinous and black venom of sin from the heart.

Be unto us, O Maiden fair, the salvation of our race, the hope and consolation of the poor, the succor of your humble servants. For grim foes assail us, enemies set their snares against us. The flesh entices with luxuries, the devil sows argument and disputes, and the world distracts us with its empty promises of wealth and honor. O Queen of Mercy! Help us in these times of anguish. Grant unto us the aid of your grace. Lest we tumble headlong into the perils which surround us, remain always with us. Be as the crystalline dawn light, while the deceptive twilight of this world relentlessly presses in upon us. O, font of salvation and source of all grace! O, true way of peace and door of mercy! Give ear to the lamentations of your servants. For danger encircles us. Illness consumes the body, while temptations torture the heart. The rain of true devotion fails to fall, fervor in prayer grows cool, and the eye of true reason waxes dim.

Prayer

O refuge of the poor! A source of mercy! To thee, the eyes of all turn with longing hope, that we may be liberated from the evils which plague us. Remain with us, as night falls. Liberate us from the darkness of sin and the shadow of death, and lead us forth into the glory of perpetual immortality. Amen.

CHAPTER 9

THE AROMATIC CROCUS FLOWER,

in the Eighth Place in the Crown of the Virgin

If I had the tongues of all peoples and the melodic voices of all the angels at my command, it would never suffice—O most holy Virgin—to express worthily your praise; for it should still remain insufficient in power and inadequate in subtlety. For the Holy Spirit gathers in you such miracles of virtues and such abundance of grace that the mind of neither humans nor angels is capable of expressing your honor in the world, your glory in the heavens, nor the opulence of the Crown which you possess as your rightful reward! As much as you deserve to be praised by all, I—a wretched sinner—desire to place in the eighth position in your magnificent crown an aromatic crocus flower. This flower is a gift most apt for you. For the crocus is golden in hue, delightful in its fragrance, wondrous in its healing powers, and most truly the source of joy to those who behold it. You likewise are golden, O Virgin Queen, with the precious gold of sanctity. For as the gold exceeds all metals in nobility and value, thus the dignity of your sanctity exceeds the merits of the saints and the prerogatives of all the angels. Therefore you are rightly exalted above all beings in heaven and on earth.

Just as on the earth there was no place of greater dignity and honor than your blessed womb, which became the temple in which you received the Son of God—even so, God has elevated you to a royal throne in heaven, towering far above all the saints! You indeed are like the aromatic crocus flower, emitting before God and humankind a most sublime fragrance. And your scent is like "the smell of a fruitful field, which the Lord has blessed."[18] Indeed, your sacred womb was such a fertile field, bringing forth a blessed harvest—our Saviour—by which the entire human race and all the angelic hosts are nourished and sustained. The perfume of your humility delights God. The fragrance of

---

[18]   Gn 28:27.

your purity entrances the angels. The aroma of your mercy refreshes the human race! Yet the scent of your sanctity also terrifies demons and fills with horror the fierce legions of hell.

You were, and you are, miraculous in virtuousness: for the virtue proceeding from you enlightens the vision, purifies the taste, refashions hearing, comforts the heart, and illumines the intellect. Often indeed—O Virgin most merciful—have you consoled the sorrowful, softened the hardened heart, strengthened the weak, revived the dead, and healed and liberated those afflicted with illness. For these, O Mistress, we rejoice in your honor and glory; we exult in your wonderful praise; we share the perfect happiness of your celestial majesty!

Hence, a certain saint has said of the joy and sweetness which you pour forth into the heart which adores you: that the holy and glorious name of MARY is verily a fragrant oil poured forth, a life-giving anointment, a balm of the heart. Let the alabaster jar be broken! Descend, O exquisite Queen, into my own garden! Light there the golden fire of love; pour forth the oil of your beauty; release the perfume of your fragrance!

PRAYER

Let Mary abide always in my memory; let the sweetness of Mary and her grace be the constant subject of my meditation; let me be ever mindful of her untiring benefits and inexhaustible charity.

O Lady, kindly accept these verses which I offer to you in honor of your glory:

> Hail, O river of mercy,
> Crystal brook of peace,
> Pellucid stream of grace,
> Limpid dew of the valley,
> Delicate blossom of modesty,
> Mother of God—
> And Mother of Mercy!
>
> Hail, O true salvation of the faithful,
> Throne of the Divine Majesty,
> Temple of Christ,
> House of the Spirit,
> Abode of the Incarnate Word,
> Road leading unto life,
> And lily of chastity.
>
> Hail, bloom of perfect beauty,

Bride of Christ, Handmaid of the Most
High.
In perfection of loveliness,
None there is who rivals thee!

We proclaim thee most venerable,
Holy of mind, and innocent of heart;
Immaculate in body,
Meek and gracious,
Pleasing to the Most High,
Beloved by God!

Those who taste thee continue yet to desire
you more,
To thirst more fervently for your incompa-
rable, sacred sweetness.
They long to love thee yet ever more
ardently, ever more devoutly,
To laud thee in song without end!
And yet for this, the human heart, mind
and tongue,
And ever all the choirs of the heavens,
Never could truly suffice.

Holy Mother of him who was both God and Man—
the glory and honor of the human race, transcending

all saints in holiness, and surpassing in radiance all the celestial power—who could ever extol thee worthily? Who could offer you fitting praises?

Because thou alone were worthy to bear God in your womb, and to suckle him as a tender infant at thy breast, our salvation lies entirely in thy hands, O glorious Lady.

Therefore look upon us with mercy, that we may securely serve God the eternal King, and thee, his blessed Mother.

O Queen of glory!

Thou indeed live and reign with God upon the throne of supernal majesty through endless eternities! Amen.

CHAPTER 10

THE IRIDESCENT AGATE STONE,

in the Ninth Place in the Crown of the Virgin

O Empress most refulgent, you are seated in the heavenly throne, crowned with glory and honor, ornate with the priceless jewels of virtue, unspeakably joyful, perfectly beautiful, and incomparably lovely! You are beautiful in virginity, *more* beautiful in humility, and *most* beautiful in the immaculate conception of the Son of God himself! You are lovely in the celestial praise you merit, lovelier in the purity of morals by which you lived, most lovely in the glory of the divine vision you enjoy.

You are beautiful indeed—for you have neither fault nor flaw, no imperfection, either of spirit or body.

50

Rather you are absolutely pure, and radiant like refined gold. The slightest tint or shadow of sin never once approached your heart, but the grace and charism of all sanctity enveloped it totally.

O most beautiful, lovely and exquisite Mistress! Accept, I pray, an agate stone, which I venture to situate in the ninth place in your crown as an adornment for you. Amongst its other power, the agate has the effect of making a person gracious; which certainly befits you, O Lady, who are more effective and potent than anything else in transforming our souls. We once languished in the darkness of sin, in the filth of concupiscence, and in the shadows of iniquity, and therefore deserved to be despised by God, even as progeny of hell. And there are indeed many inflated by pride, blackened with avarice, bloody through wrath, foul through lust and luxury, jaundiced through gluttony, livid through envy and bloated by sloth.

But when it was pleasing to him who had chosen you from your mother's womb, your immaculate heart was moved with pity for us. Then—by the assistance of your maternal hand—we were led from the domain of darkness to sanctity's realm of infinite light. Vices came to be detested and abstinence to be embraced. Sinful desire was extinguished, and virtue sprang once more to life. For "you open your hand, and fill all living beings with blessings."[19] Once the seed of grace is sown within us, the proud become humble; the avaricious, generous; the greedy, temperate; the lustful, chaste; the wrathful, charitable; and the slothful, industrious. And thus we—who had been the offspring of darkness—are transformed into children of the Light and co-heir with Christ of the heavenly kingdom. Glory to God in the highest! For he graciously has furnished us with such a needed and beloved Protectress as you, O Mother of mercy, who were granted, by the grace of God;

> to empty the infernal dungeons of hell,
> to illuminate the world,
> to enhance the lustre of heaven,
> to enrich paradise,
> to crush the devil,
> to seize the prey from the jaws of the devouring lion;
> to lead sinners to repentance.

O Mary, full of grace, refulgent Virgin, aureate, pure and flawless, consecrated as the dwelling place of Christ, vessel of glory and beauty precious in the eyes

---

[19]   Ps 144:4.

of the highest King! O innocent maiden, blessed by the Holy Spirit, protected by the holy angels, adored by the seraphim, adorned with infinite graces and virtues!

Turn to me your sweet, gracious eyes of mercy, O Mistress, resplendent and luminous. Visit me, who languish in infirmity. Care for me, afflicted with suffering. Console me, who weep and mourn. Grant to me a devout heart and an enlightened mind, that I may comprehend the greatness of your goodness, the magnificence of your purity, the depths of your wisdom, and the sanctity of your body and soul. O Highest Empress, look down from the exalted heights of your majesty and shed the splendor of the light of your grace upon the darkness of my soul, repair my wounded heart, and inflame my being with your love!

PRAYER

I pray to thee, O Mary: that your holy virginity may render me chaste; that your motherhood may grant me increase in virtue; that your humility may make me humble; that your sanctity may make me contrite; that your mercy may make me worthy of eternal life; and, that you permit me to serve as a devout poet of praise for as long as this earthly life abides!

For, alas, my body is afflicted with torments. My soul is almost broken by temptations. Internal peace and sweetness have vanished from my heart. O holy Queen of Virgins! Grant solace and succor unto thy supplicant. Behold the tears of one crying out to thee. Remain with me, O Mary, since the dense gloom of despair begins to envelop me.

O Virgin immaculate, O Queen crowned by the hand of the Most High, grant that this tearful soul that beseeches thee may one day become truly meek and humble and genuinely contrite for its sins, and thus may enter into the felicity of eternal life and join the noble ranks of the blessed saints and angels in heaven! Amen.

CHAPTER 11

THE STAR OF THE SEA,

in the Tenth Place in the Crown of the Virgin Mary

That we should fervently praise and bless you, O Holy Mother of Christ, we are constantly advised by the word of Sacred Scripture. We are instructed by the examples of the saints, encouraged by the many generous benefits you grant us, and inspired by your miraculous graces. For you bore God himself to mortals. You achieved true peace for this world. You overcame and conquered the devil, and you brought restoration to the human race. Through your unfailing intercession, you obtain for your devotees every imaginable boon and blessing, both in heaven and on earth! You are, in truth:

the most noble throne of the Holy Trinity;

the beauteous and virginal bridal chamber
of the Incarnate Word;
the most precious jewel adorning the crown
of the Eternal Emperor;
the most beloved daughter of the Highest
Father;
the most adored bride of the Holy Spirit;
the Mistress and Queen of both angels and
humankind.

You are—in yourself—an entire and wondrous choir of heavenly harmony, filled with supernal wisdom, resplendent with holy radiance, brilliant in all virtue, perfect in beauty! You shine amidst an array of price-less, fiery gemstones—that is amongst the glory of all the hosts of angels and archangels. In sanctity, you are exalted above all others in the paradise of God, as a noble cedar towering above the other trees of a viridescent[20] and majestic forest. You are the highest of the Seraphim, winged with six snow-plumed pinions. Inflamed with the Creator's love, you soar in an endless flight of rapture, in the beatific contemplation of the majesty of the Divinity.

---

[20]   greenish

Therefore I—although unworthy—am desirous of honoring such an illustrious Lady. Hence I place in the tenth position in your crown the Star of the Sea. This light faithfully directs the wandering sailor and all those who strive to navigate across the perilous waves of the endless ocean of life. It encourages them and guides them and finally leads them to the harbor of safety they desire. You, O Mistress, are indeed this star! You, among the waves of temptation and the pain of affliction, always direct and guide us. You offer us much-needed aid and assistance in times of trial and lead our souls to the harbor of God's salvation. Let all your devout servants and supplicants implore your protection and guidance, O true Star of the Sea!

PRAYER

O my soul, in times of peril, in moments of uncertainty, look towards your guiding Star. Call upon the name of Mary; let it never recede from your heart, let it never depart from your lips. For, following her faithfully, you shall never stray.

Calling upon her, you shall never despair. With her as Protectress, you shall never fear. With her guiding you, you shall never grow weary. With her as your leader, you shall arrive safely at your celestial homeland.

O Mary, grant that this may happen through your glorious merits and holy intercession, by the grace of your most blessed and Divine Son, with whom you live and reign forever and ever. Amen.

CHAPTER 12

THE JASPER STONE,

Placed in the Eleventh Position in the Crown of Our Lady

May you be blessed, O Mother of Christ Jesus, our Lord—Mother of Mercy, and Lady of all consolation, who console us in all our tribulations. May the holy name of your glory be blessed, praised, and exalted until the end of time. O, Door of paradise! O, Handmaid of grace and servant of the Holy Spirit! O, Mistress of all wisdom and divine contemplation! O, best teacher of the poverty and humility of Christ! You are more noble than the patriarchs in faith and patience, more perceptive than the prophets in knowledge and insight, higher than the apostles in perfection of sanctity. You surpassed all martyrs in enduring suffering for Christ and excelled all the saints in works of virtue. In purity you surpassed all other virgins, and the angels and archangels you excelled in the abundance of your grace. You are more radiant than the cherubim in splendor of wisdom and more illustrious than the seraphim in ardor of love! Truly, you transcend all other created beings in wisdom, sanctity, and grace, and none there is who rivals you.

Therefore, I—a humble sinner yearning to pay fitting homage to you—place in the eleventh position in your noble crown a precious jasper stone. The jasper is a stone filled with mysterious virtues and most exquisite in its wondrous variety of mingled colors. It has the medicinal power of stemming the flow of blood from wounds. This is indeed well suited as an ornament to your holy crown, O Mistress; for you are ornate with a splendid variety of virtues, and infused with the combined powers of virginity and sanctity. And you bring to mortals the most efficacious and salubrious effect of stemming the blood which flows from the woundedness of our fallen nature—which is to say, of restraining the sinful desires and concupiscence of the flesh.

You are most wondrous in your fortitude, most virtuous in your righteousness, most loving in your charity, most radiant in your wisdom, most penetrating in your intelligence, most kind in your mercy. In prosperity and exaltation, you were humble; in adversity, you were strong and unwavering; in your sanctity, you were and are truly sublime! The freshness of virginity constantly imbues your celestial body with beauty, grace, and vigor, while the strength of your faith imbues your immortal mind with youthfulness and energy. By your virtues, you bring healing to the wounds of our sinfulness. You alone have the power to wash away whatever unclean and hidden desires lurk within us.

PRAYER

Therefore, O most stunning Maiden, and true lover of virginity, extinguish in me the burning flames of unholy desire. By the supernal dew of your grace, create in me a flowering garden of purity, where the white blooms of chastity may flourish.

In all my prayer, meditation, reading, and work, may my mind be conscious of the delight of your angelic presence, consoling, directing, and guiding me unfailingly. Anoint my heart with the priceless anointment of your sweetness, that I may know and desire the heavenly flavor of your love and the celestial delight of your friendship.

But I—a miserable and blind sinner—frequently am led astray by exterior things. I become distracted and

oblivious of your love, seeking vain and empty consolation in the delights of the flesh. Thus I often find
myself enmeshed in transitory and fallen things, in my
thoughts, deeds, speech, and emotions.

But you, O Mistress, loving fervently that which is
celestial, dwell in a distant realm of inaccessible light!
You exult in heaven whilst I languish on earth. You love
that which is incorruptible and eternal while I yearn for
fleeting and transitory things, in which there is no real
substance but vanity, misery, and affliction of spirit.

What more need I say? You are holy, pious, and just;
I am wicked, vengeful, and profane. You are light itself;
I am blind. You are life; I am dead. You are pure joy; I
am nothing but misery. So I cry out to thee:

> O Mother of my Creator, bring me to life!
> O Mother of my Redeemer, redeem me!
> O Mother of my Savior, save me!

O most glorious Lady, I beg thee—lest the lethal temptations of the flesh totally overcome me—gently hold
my heart, direct my thoughts, guard my soul—so that,
through the power of thy chaste love, I may cling to
thee more perfectly and in the richness of thy sweetness
and grace, I may at last rest secure.

CHAPTER 13

THE ROSE OF SPRING,

in the Twelfth Place in the Crown of the Virgin

O Queen Divinely consecrated, you are nothing less than a seraphic throne from which shines forth with refulgent splendor the entire majesty, glory, virtue, and magnificence of the Holy Trinity! And therefore the whole assembly of angels and archangels—together with the brilliant assembly of cherubim and seraphim, and the exalted communion of all the saints—praise and glorify you with endless devotion. For that which lay broken and cast down was restored through you, O Mistress of grace!

And so, with voices of supernal sweetness, mingled in waves of celestial harmony, they proclaim to you a

Divine hymn, infinite in praise, unceasing in veneration. Thus do they sing:

> "Who is this who comes forth, even as the
>   dawn,
> beautiful as the moon, radiant as the sun,
> as awesome as an insuperable army arrayed
>   in might?"[21]

When you were born, O Virgin, you arose like a glowing dawn. For your birth marked the beginning of the day of grace and the end of the dark night of sin and infidelity. And you indeed possessed the beauty of the moon, filled with the grace of the conception of the incarnate Word. You brought forth the Sun of justice, Jesus Christ, and so you yourself were the morning of our salvation, putting to flight the darkness of our sin. And just as the ray departing from the sun does not diminish its coruscant brilliance—so, the Sun of justice and Son of God being born from you did not violate or diminish your virginal purity. Through you, O Mother of mercy, the eternal rays of Divine splendor shone forth to the whole world!

---

[21] Song of Songs 6:9.

And you are indeed like an army, arrayed for battle,[22] for you appeared with all the angels exulting, all the saints rejoicing, all the flags of virtue flying. All the stars of the heavens stand ready and obedient at your behest.

O Lady miraculous—resplendent with the brilliance of the sun, exquisite with the loveliness of the moon! Accept the rose of spring which I offer you, that it may be positioned in the twelfth place in your noble coronet. For the rose is called the "flower of flowers" for its surpassing excellence. It is pleasing to the sight, entrancing in its fragrance, and powerful in its medicinal properties. And all of these properties are to be found in you, O gracious Virgin.

But you are not merely like the earthly rose—which springs up and then soon withers. Rather, you are the rose of paradise, which is held lovingly in the hand of the King of heaven! For you are the perfect bloom of virginal beauty and the Queen of all virgins, the Empress of all holy maidens, unmatched in radiance and peerless in immortal chastity. And so you sit, triumphant, upon a sublime throne of imperial dignity. For you are of matchless beauty—in the sight of God,

---

[22]   See Song of Songs 6:10.

through your faith; and in the sight of angels, through your purity; and in the sight of sinful mortals, through your compassionate mercy.

It was, indeed, the fragrance of your vernal sweetness that caused the Son of God himself to descend from his heavenly throne to this earthly realm. It was your perfection that compelled him to dwell as a guest in your virginal womb. And so a devout poet once fittingly wrote:

> The sun outshines the moon,
> And the moon surpasses the stars;
> Even so, Mother Mary exceeds
> All other created beings.
> Hail, Mother of mercy!
> Hail, abode of the Trinity!
> For thou hast prepared within thyself
> The dwelling place of Christ himself,
> The home of the Word incarnate,
> The resting place of the Son of God.

Your healing power helps us in our infirmity and adversity, refreshes us in our labors, and consoles us in all sorrow. Indeed, it is said truly that your mercy, O Holy Virgin, is our surest aid in all peril and our best defence against all affliction.

Prayer

Since you are graced with such a multitude of heavenly privileges, illumine—O most beautiful Light—my vision. Thus may I behold more clearly thy beauty! Heal my taste, that I may taste thy sweetness; renew my smelling, that I may experience thy fragrance. Inflame my heart with thy most holy wisdom, that I may contemplate thee with wonder, love thee with fervor, venerate thee with true devotion, and cling to thee with fidelity!

Stand by me, O Lady, while I pray to you devoutly, and mediate upon you, and read about you, and speak of you, and anxiously send up my sighs to you. For your perfume refreshes me. The thought of you brings me comfort, and your sweetness restores me. Your very presence consoles me. And your guidance faithfully leads me along the narrow path and straight road which leads to the divine light of heaven. Amen.

Chapter 14

THE PRECIOUS RUBY,

in the Thirteenth Place in the
Crown of the Virgin

O royal Virgin, adorned by the virtues of all gem-stones, decorated with the jewellery of all the graces, clothed in the raiment of all justice, adored through heaven and earth for your incomparable beauty! Your grace so attracted the heart of the highest King that he descended from his celestial throne and hastened madly to your embrace! If therefore, God himself, the Creator of all things visible and invisible, so desired your beauty, how much more should we—who were once condemned but now, through you, are saved—how passionately and devotedly should we love you? With what great praise shall we extol you? For you are indeed more radiant than the sun itself and the most beauteous of all womankind.

And since you are so exquisite, resplendent, and bright, and truly as sparkling as crystal, I entreat you to accept the gift of a precious ruby gemstone, which I place in the thirteenth position in your holy crown. This rare stone illuminates darkness and strikes the eyes of those who behold it with a forceful and irresistible luminosity. And this is indeed the effect you have upon humanity, O unique Mother of Christ. For who could express the light of mercy which you have brought to a darkened world? What tongue could suffice to describe your miracles and wonders, the marvels and glories, the signs and portents which bring about—for the healing of souls and bodies, for the encouragement of the righteous, and for the correction of those going astray? The depths of your mercy, indeed, can never be fully known or comprehended.

It is therefore rightly the delight of all Christians to praise and bless you, O Mary. And whenever your name MARY is uttered, heads are bowed in reverence, hearts are filled with the fire of hope and love, and tears of contrition and devotion flow forth from humble eyes. O name more splendid than the sun, more fragrant than the finest cinnamon! At the sound of this name the world rejoices, the heavens smile, the angels celebrate, and the saints exult! Yet the forces of hell tremble, and the devil is thwarted.

For whenever anyone sincerely turns the eyes of their heart to contemplate the perfection of your sanctity, or the depths of your wisdom, or the magnificence of your beauty, they are immediately and unfailing given the grace of new hope in the mind, joy in the soul, and peace in the heart—and, indeed, whatever spiritual graces are needful.

PRAYER

O most merciful Mary, who breathe life into those who are dying and health into those who perish! You are light for the blind, solace to those who despair, and consolation to those who weep! From the fathomless depths of the treasury of your mercies, pour out to me—I beg you—joy of heart, happiness of soul, and clarity of mind. Be unto me life and well-being, the peace of my heart, and the delight of my soul!

O most resplendent Star of the Sea, Mother most compassionate! Guide me and defend me against all foes and perils so that, helped by your grace and assisted by your mercy, I may be purged from all vices and liberated from all adversity. Thus may I pass through the

present life unharmed and arrive safely at the life which
has no end! Amen.

CHAPTER 15

THE SUN,

the Most Brilliant and Powerful of All
Heavenly Bodies,
in the Fourteenth Place,
Illuminating the Entire Crown

O Mary—unbroken seal of chastity, pure lily of virginity, most beautiful of women, more delightful than all the angels, more holy than all the saints, richer than all created being in abundance of grace! Seraphim hail you, God the Father sanctifies you, God the Holy Spirit shades you protectingly, God the Son chooses you as his betrothed! The sanctity of your soul conceived God through faith. The purity of your womb bore him. The virginity of your body brought him forth into the world.

O glorious Lady, and more than glorious! O praise-worthy Virgin, and more than praiseworthy! Who is able to express your wonders or worthily to tell of your merits? For you gave joy to heaven, you bore God himself to the earth, you opened the river of celestial peace to a troubled world.

Through you, O Queen of heaven:

> Light is given to the blind,
> Sure faith bestowed to doubtful hearts,
> Vices are brought under control,
> Demons are confounded,
> Ravenous hell is deprived of its prey.
> heaven is enriched,
> The poor are nourished,
> The weak are sustained,
> The humble are raised up,
> The gates of paradise are unlocked.

Therefore the patriarchs long for you. The apostles embrace you. The Evangelists reverence you. The martyrs venerate you. The preachers proclaim your glory. The choirs of virgins rejoice around you. The angels glorify you, and all of creation exalts you! Even I—a lowly sinner—seek to contribute in some way to your glory and honor. And so I venture to offer to you the sun itself, the most radiant and potent of the celestial bodies, to be positioned in the fourteenth place in your noble crown. Thence it may freely shed its lustre upon you, bathing you in incomparable light!

For the sun possess the highest position in the celestial sphere, and the greatest sureness in its daily motion across the sky. It brings forth the greatest fertility in its effect upon the earth, while bestowing the gift of light more brilliantly than any other star. Similarly you, O Mistress, are raised up most high of all, by virtue of your sanctity and singular purity. Your immaculate heart is raised up to the uppermost rank in the seraphic courts, closest to the inaccessible light of the unseen Father. With the gentle eyes of a dove you lovingly contemplate his luminous divinity. With the fearless and penetrating eyes of an eagle you boldly perceive the depths of his majesty.

And your every action proceeds with the greatest sureness—with unfailing certainty and assurance, born of true piety. Like the sun, you traverse the earthly globe, attentively beholding the needs of the poor, the anxious sighs of youth, the pains of the elderly, the lamentations of widows, the sufferings of the sick, and the prayers poured forth to you and your Holy Son from faithful hearts everywhere. As the gracious Protectress of the entire race, you help the afflicted, the sorrowful, and those who have lost hope. You do this by the divine grace of your mercy and by your powerful intercession with your noble Son, Jesus—the King of kings and Lord of lords!

And—like the warming sun which causes the earth to flourish with springtide verdancy—so you make souls once barren to become fruitful. For who is able to moisten the dry heart like you? Or who is able so to warm the mind, frozen with despair or cynicism? All the good things, which God's supreme Majesty has decreed to bestow on us, he has decreed to bestow through your intercession and agency. He has committed to your maternal hands the entire treasuries of his golden wisdom, the precious gemstones of his virtues, and the glowing ornaments of his graces. Through you—radiant as the sun, as gentle as the dawn—the fruits of blessings spring forth from their divine source.

How many are the former thieves you have led to repentance? How many are the reformed prostitutes you have converted to chastity? How many of the avaricious have you made generous, and to how many drunkards have you taught sobriety? How many of the wrathful have you tempered by the example of your patience and mercy, and how many of the lustful have you restrained by the example of your immaculate purity?

Utterly radiant and splendid you stand, clothed in light as with a vestment, and crowned with twelve glowing stars! As the refulgent sun dawns with golden radiance, so you adorn and illuminate the celestial Jerusalem, the city of paradise, the abode of saints, angels and God himself! And therefore the ranks of the angels are struck with wonder, and the legions of seraphim stand awestruck before you, O Mary! For you are indeed the very perfection of sanctity, the complete plenitude of grace, and the luminous fire of God's ardent love.

PRAYER

O Lady of grace, since such marvels are told of thee, pour forth, I beseech thee, thy love into my heart. Show unto me the angelic beauty of thy countenance, splendid as the noontide sun. Grant that, at the hour of my death, I may surrender my spirit—joyful in thy radiance, and secure in the hope of unfading glory. Amen.

CHAPTER 16

THE EMERALD,

in the Fifteenth Place in the Crown of the Virgin

O wisest, golden throne of the Holy Trinity,
  O most worthy ivory seat of Jesus Christ,
    the Son of God!
  O virginal Mother, and motherly Virgin,
  O most beautiful of brides,
  O Lady who—after God himself—
are my salvation, my hope, my consolation!

Amidst the turbulent waves of this life, you, O Mary, are my secure anchor. Amid the shipwrecks of this world, you are the safe harbor to which I flee. You are my help in adversities, my guide in perplexities, my secret joy in times of trial, and my refreshment in labor. Show yourself to me, O daughter of the highest King, for you are the delight of my soul, the light of my mind, the peace and serenity of my heart!

May this mortal race reverently behold you—you, who are the jubilation of the angels, the reparation of the lost, the crown of the lilies-white host of holy virgins. May the children of Adam come truly to know you—you, who are the hope of all penitents, the illumination of all holy minds, the font of all true goodness, and the immortal victory of the saints!

Appear unto me, for you are the consoler of my soul, the healer of my heart, and my way to final salvation. Let me embrace you with holy and chaste desire, O Virgin—lily of chastity, delicate flower of virginal purity!

And because I have resolved to honor your loveliness and beauty, my Queen, I ask that you deign to accept an emerald, a most precious gem, which I will dare to place in the fifteenth position in your glorious crown. For the emerald is a most valuable and rare stone, soothing in its intense greenness, and most pleasing to the eyes which gaze deeply into it. To this you may well be compared, O Virgin—you, who are our true morning star. For what created thing is there which was ever more pleasing to God and more soothing to humankind?

You are not only more precious than all gemstones but, indeed, than all mortals, than the sun, moon, and stars of heaven, than all the ranks of the angels and saints! You are the verdant secret tree in the centre of the garden of paradise, adorned with rarest flowers, robed with glowing green foliage, and bearing luscious fruit. The viridescent radiance of your soul illuminates the eyes of the mind and the body. The fragrance of the rare flowers of your heart raises up the dead, while the sweetness of your divine fruit—the blessed fruit of your womb, our Lord Jesus Christ—brings hope to those who despair.

PRAYER

O Mary, enlighten the eyes of my mind with your glowing green splendor, and let your sweet fragrance of freshness fill my soul with new life. May I possess you totally in my heart, as a rare gem; for you are the light of the world, the glory of the Church, the joy of the heavenly Jerusalem. Pour out your burning love into every fibre of my being, that I may be inflamed with praising, glorifying, and proclaiming you. Let your sweet voice whisper gently into my ear, O Queen of peace! Reveal to me the beauty of your face, and then my soul shall truly have found its salvation.

And kindly hear, in the abundance of your mercy, the ceaseless laments and restless cries which express the pains and anxieties by which our poor human race is afflicted. For in our days, peace has vanished from the earth, our people languish from a famine of true Faith, and murder and avarice dominate the world. Harvests and crops fail. Fertile fields wither into deserts. But vices spring up more and more every day, and new sins are added to old ones. And hence natural disasters are everywhere multiplied.

Piety and mercy have become rare, and worldliness has infected even many of those who profess to be religious. Fraud and deception abound, and the Church has become the target of assaults and insults. See, O most merciful Mother, how many are the miseries into which human nature has fallen, how great are the adversities faced by your Son's holy Catholic Church, and how faithless our world has become!

Gentle Mother, may your tender mercy condole us in our misery. May you serve as an advocate for us on the Day of Judgement, averting the justified indignation of the Eternal Father. May the impieties of our world be subdued and peace be restored. May religious life flourish with new vigor and Faith be restored to the hearts of humanity—that we may give more fitting praise and glory to our Lord Jesus Christ, together with the Father and the Holy Spirit, who live and reigns for ever and ever. Amen.

CHAPTER 17

THE VIOLET,

the Most Beautiful of All Flowers, in the Sixteenth Place in the Crown of the Virgin

Y̲ou, O Mistress, are the most exquisite of all women, and the most lovely treasure of all creation—of purity inviolate and of chastity immaculate. You are the most beautiful of all the daughters of Jerusalem; that is, of all those saintly women who have consecrated themselves to virginity for the sake of Jesus. For, while they are privileged to preserve the purity of virginity, you alone also rejoice in the fruitfulness of motherhood—and not motherhood only, but motherhood of God himself!

You are indeed beautiful in chaste love, but more beautiful in your works of mercy, and most beautiful of all in the virginal conception and bearing of Christ our Lord. You are lovely in virginity, lovelier yet in humility, but most lovely of all in radiant charity. Your sweet disposition makes you enchanting. The sanctity of your life makes you resplendent, and your royal majesty renders you glorious! Surrounded by angelic powers, your immaculate heart was perfectly untouched—except by divine love. Hence you remained eternally inviolate in body and mind. You are the unfading Star of the Sea, the illuminating guide closest to the peak of heaven, to whom Christians sigh longingly as they navigate through the fluctuating waves of this life.

That I may have some claim to be guided by your most holy light, I offer to you, O my love, the most gorgeous of all flowers, a violet, to position in the sixteenth place of your royal diadem. The violet is of richest purple hue, wonderful in its fragrance, and endowed with healing powers. Well does this flower befit your crown, for it faithfully strives to imitate your virtues. You are indeed a violet of purity, of modesty, and of chastity; and a violet of sweetness, of sanctity, and of love.

For the purple shade of this flower matches the limpid hue of the clear and serene sky, reflecting your elevation to the things of heaven and your soul's saturation with God's celestial light. Your heart, impelled by ardent praise of the Creator, makes its dwelling place amongst the highest constellations. It is held fast there by love, in the closest proximity to the sublime throne of God himself.

And, like the violet, your fragrance imparts a wonderful joy to those devoted to you, while your very touch heals all those who call upon you. And therefore a certain saint has rightly declared: "You are the best guardian of the human race, and the unique medicine for the afflicted heart."

Prayer

O cloud of fulvid light,
Sublime in astral height,
O blooming branch of grace,
The glory of our race.

Made fruitful by the dew
Which Love rained down on you,
Make tender stony hearts;
Your grace to us impart!

You are true Wisdom's throne,
Of luminance unknown,
The cedar tree divine,

The verdant, fertile vine.

God's pardon for us seek,
O, Maiden mild and meek.
O, snow-white lily flower,
And Queen of untold power!

O, Empress of the skies,
Delight of weary eyes,
Of paradise the door,
The refuge of the poor.

Our God's most cherished Mother,
Surpassing every other!
Release us from our fears,
In this dark vale of tears;

Preserve us from despair,
Protect us by your care.
And help us to be true,
To Jesus, and to you!
Amen.

CHAPTER 18

THE AMETHYST,

in the Seventeenth Place in the Crown of the Virgin

Hail, O holy Mother of God, golden resting place of the Savior of the world—you who are like the light of dawn, illuminating the hearts of all the saints! You yourself are the greatest teacher and example of virtue, the rule of the cloister, the word of peace, the sword of the spirit, and the shield of holy victory. Your virtuous power irradiates the heavens and brings the purest and highest of joys to the angels. Yet it terrifies demons and makes the minions of hell tremble! You are the imperial throne of God, the seat of the Holy Trinity, the resting place of our Lord Jesus—consecrated, sanctified, and adorned by the Holy Spirit. On earth

you are adored. In heaven you are crowned and venerated as unrivalled Queen!

You bind up the proud and strong, yet break asunder
the bonds of captivity for the humble. You are truly the
Mother of virtue, the destroyer of sin, the secret key
to the celestial Kingdom, the radiant mirror of chastity. Hail, O lovely Virgin!—you who are the nexus
between heaven and earth, prefigured by the patriarchs,
foretold by the prophets, proclaimed by the apostles,
expounded by the holy doctors!

And since you are proclaimed and praised by such
luminaries, and acclaimed and revered by such a ver-
itable multitude, it is only right that whatever I can
give—albeit it very small and poor—I should humbly
offer for the glorification of your majesty. O gracious
Mary, deign to accept therefore, I beg you, a precious
amethyst stone, to be inserted in the seventeenth position in your radiant crown. From thence it will show
forth well its distinctive lustre.

The amethyst combines, in its enchanting hue, the
colors of both the violet and the rose. And for this wondrous mixture, it fittingly is placed in your noble diadem. For you indeed combine the fragrance and beauty
of the delicate violet with that of the splendid rose. In
the violet is your humility commended, while the rose

bespeaks of your marvellous love. For out of humility, you declared yourself to be the lowly handmaid of the Lord. And for the sake of fervid love, he gave to you the most sublime glory and honor.

Thus you excel not only all mortals but even the celestial legions of angels, archangels, the puissant ranks of thrones, dominions, and powers, and even the exalted and luminous company of cherubim and seraphim. In miraculous chastity, you transcend all holy virgins. In your virginal motherhood, you presented to the world its one true Redeemer and Savior. You surpass all martyrs in your triumphant victory. No deception of the tempter could enter within the virginal cloister of your mind. No blandishment of that seducer of souls could make your constancy waver. No spear of the enemy could threaten your insuperable fortitude.

You excelled all the apostles through the excellence of your sanctity and the plenitude of your grace, in your pure charity to your neighbor, in your penetration of the mysteries of Jesus Christ, and in your experience of the celestial glories of the eternal Father. You were stronger than all patriarchs and prophets in your faith, hope, and patience. You were more perspicacious and profound in your grasp of all things past, present, and future, and in your understanding of the arcane secrets of the Deity. You rank far above all celestial spirits and all angelic beings in your perfect purity of mind, in the splendor of your wisdom, in the tranquillity of your peace, and in the ardor of your love!

Prayer

O most delightful Lady—since God has placed all good things in thy hands—I entreat thee, that thou may kindly hear my prayer, and by your intercession, may obtain for me peace and clemency.

Virgin of most splendid glory,
Blest by God's great Paraclete,
Peaceful dove, so gently sighing,
Rule our hearts and guide our feet.

Guard us from all foe and peril,
Look on us, in tears forlorn,
Maiden, robed in golden mercy,
With the gems of grace adorned.

Save us from the snares of Satan,
Striving to enslave our race,
Thou, the throne of holy Wisdom,
Thou, the vessel of all grace.

Virgin-spouse of highest heaven,
Bond connecting God and man,
Arc of promises unbroken,
Lead us with maternal hand.

As the hopeful light of morning,
As the dawn-star drawing nigh,
In the hour of death be with us,
Make our souls to glory fly!

CHAPTER 19

THE BRIGHT AND REFULGENT MOON,

in the Eighteenth Place in the Crown of the Virgin

Rejoice and be glad, O daughter of Zion, exalted Virgin, lily of paradise! For in you all the hosts of heaven are filled with indescribable joy. You are the reconciliation of the world, the epitome of peace, and the way of salvation. The Savior loved you in a singular fashion and united himself to you through his incarnation in your womb, commending to you the fullness of his grace. And therefore angels praise you, dominions adore you, principalities and powers pay you homage. The blessed seraphim, with extended wings, exult with rapture in your presence! And even I, though the most lowly and unworthy of sinners, am inspired with a desire to please you. Accordingly, I place the Moon—full and radiant—in the eighteenth rank in your crown, that it may illuminate it with the pearl-like effulgence of its silver light.

The moon, indeed, receives its own light from the supreme light and source of all light, the sun, and thus serves to illuminate the night. It is mild and lovely, casting refreshing dew upon the earth,[23] while exposing thieves in the hours of darkness and repelling them from their nefarious deeds. These traits are all reflective of you, most splendid Lady! Therefore this heavenly body is befittingly located amongst the adornments of your holy diadem.

For you gaze upon the splendor of the true Sun; that is, the throne of the Divine Majesty with its incomparable and intense solar radiance. You reflect God's magnificence in your own being. But you do this in mild form, gentle and yet clear—communicating and transmitting its light faithfully, yet subtly. And thus you illumine the night of our sorrow, you put to flight the impulse to sin, and refresh the barren soul with spiritual dew.

---

23   It was believed in the Middle Ages that the rising of the moon at night cast dew upon the earth.

O most holy Virgin of virgins, most blessed resting place of the celestial Majesty! With how much fervor ought we to praise your glory! With how many tears and prayers should we implore your aid! At your name, every knee shall bend—of beings terrene, celestial, and of the netherworld—and all tongues shall profess you, O Mother of our Lord Jesus Christ. For in you is reflected the glory of God the Father! You are seated in tranquil glory at the right hand of your beloved Spouse and beloved Son. You are adorned with the radiance of the stars and surrounded by choirs of holy virgins. You are exalted by the multitude of saints and angels—amongst lilies of perpetual freshness, in the courts of paradise! May your Divine Son, our Saviour, lead us there, where we may rejoice in your presence. Until then, graciously be pleased to accept, O great Lady, my humble song which follows:

Prayer

Hail, O Throne of Majesty,
Lily of humility,
Fragrant rose of chastity,
Mirror of Divinity!

Hail, O Temple filled with light,

Moon of beauty glowing bright,
Putting earthly fears to flight,
Shining through sin's darksome night!

O, refreshing crystal rain,
Which all sweetness does contain,
Making flourish grace-filled grain,
Bringing solace for our pain.

Mystic, fastened treasure chest
In which God himself took rest!
Angels serve at thy behest;
Seraphim declare thee blest!

Gracious Maiden, Queen of peace,
From our woes, grant us release,
Make our love for thee increase;
May thy praises never cease!
Amen.

CHAPTER 20

THE PERIDOT GEMSTONE,

in the Nineteenth Place in the
Crown of the Virgin

Rejoice, Virgin daughter of Zion! Exult, Mother and Bride of Christ! For the Lord God is your eternal light, and your own Son, the Son of God, is your glory. The voice of the heavens resounds with your praise, and the starry firmament sings to you an endless canticle of glory. And this is only fitting, for by your incomparable light both heaven and earth are illuminated. Who is there, O Mother of mercy, who is excluded from the holy sweetness of your clemency? By your merits, the devils themselves are confounded, hell is deprived of its prey, the whole world is enlightened, the angels dance for joy, and paradise is filled with rejoicing beyond all words!

What thanks am I—an unworthy sinner—able to give to you, O most awesome Queen? In your womb are hidden the divine mysteries. In your immaculate heart, the secrets of heaven are carefully guarded. In your soul, the wisdom of God is magnificently enthroned. By no trace of sin were you stained. By no fault or failing were you blemished. Therefore you received God himself into your womb! You clothed him with flesh and bore him to the world. And because you presented this most precious and most delightful gift to humanity—your glorious Son—I offer to you, for your praise and glory, a rare and precious peridot gemstone. Permit me to place this gemstone in the nineteenth position in your noble crown of honor, O Mary.

This unusually colored gem combines the fulvid shade of gold, with that of a greenish-tinged ocean. In the tints of gold, reverent mercy is expressed; while the shade of the sea expresses the bitterness of tearful sorrow. Just as gold excels all other metals in value and purity, so mercy exceeds all other good works in the sight of our merciful God. And you exceeded all others, O Mary, in your mercy, extended towards all those who suffer the bitterness of tribulation—to the poor, the afflicted, the desolate, the broken-hearted.

For verily you yourself knew the most bitter of sorrows—even as the sufferings of your Divine Son became a sword that pierced your own immaculate heart.

Prayer

O Mary, turn your most holy and merciful gaze towards me, a wretched sinner, totally lacking in grace! Illuminate my spirit, inflame my heart, revive my soul, and renew my mind. Merciful Mother, refresh me; prudent Virgin, instruct me; light of my life, guide me; my strength, bring me comfort!

Let my actions be directed through you, and let my intentions and thoughts be governed by your goodness. Let you light enter into my heart, and your love into my soul, so that I may sweetly know, taste, and sense your presence with me at all times.

You, most holy Virgin, are the true ark of the Covenant, adorned with purest gold, in which are hidden all the treasures of the grace and mercy of God—on the exterior, gilded with virtues, and on the interior lined with the gold of innocence and piety.

You are perfectly faultless in mind, and totally beautiful in exterior graces, radiant with the brilliance of Divine light. You are the true temple of the Lord. His omnipotence is expressed in your charity, and his wisdom is revealed in your humility, his kindness in your virtue, his strength in your faith, his purity in your virginity, and his sanctity in your actions and demeanor. You are the life of the world, the healing medicine to afflicted souls, the Tree of Life in the centre of the garden of paradise! You are the glory of the world, the pillar of heaven, the firmament of virtue, the sword which overcomes the devil, the force which makes hell tremble! You extinguish sinful lusts, make the fruits of virtue to germinate, strengthen the weak, give sight to the blind, feed the hungry, protect the poor, and lead the dying to the glory of paradise—which the death and resurrection of your most blessed Son, JESUS, has won for us! Amen.

CHAPTER 21

HERE, THE BLESSED VIRGIN IS PRAISED,

and a Sunflower Is Placed in the Twentieth Place in Her Crown

Like the sun arising upon the world from the realms above, thus does your visage, O Virgin Mary, shine upon the entire celestial palace of the heavens. And this beautiful face so captivated the King of kings and Lord of lords that he accepted the woes of our mortality and bestowed upon us the riches of his divinity. And thus you are rightly proclaimed to be the cause of our gaining all God's blessings—not only life that lasts forever but life that is filled with joy, virtue, and sanctity!

In your own gracious person you give us a perfect example of all good works. You obtain for us from God all spiritual charisms of grace. Through your mediation,

the sweetness of God's mercy, the kindness of his forgiveness, and the fruitfulness of his grace flow down to
us like dew. Through you, divine spiritual gifts are given
and the mysteries of heaven are revealed. Through you,
the saving sacrament of the Church was born. Through
you, joy is given to angels, salvation to the human race,
and peace to the world!

> Thou, the light of yearning hearts,
> Star which highest joy imparts;
> You console all those who cry,
> Kindly hear each pleading sigh;
>
> Filled with fragrances most sweet,
> Which the longing senses greet;
> As the azure sapphire, bright;
> As the diamond's clearer light,
>
> As the emerald's glowing hue,
> As pure gold, refined and true,
> Precious, rare, beyond compare,
> Such art thou, O Maiden fair!
>
> As the cedar, tow'ring tall,
> Raised, majestic, over all,
> Thus art thou, O Queen supreme,
> God's true joy, each heart's best dream.

Therefore, I, a sinner, offer to your glory and honor, out of my poverty, a sunflower—a bloom sweetly redolent with fragrance and pleasing—which I place in the twentieth position in your crown. It is known as a "sunflower" because it seeks ardently and follows faithfully the sun. When the sun shines above it, it rejoices in splendor; yet when the sun disappears, it withdraws itself sadly. To this sunflower, O Mary, I compare thee!

For when the Sun of Justice, our Lord and Savior, entered your womb in mortal flesh, how greatly you rejoiced! Your soul magnified the Lord in an embrace of ecstatic love. Yet, when the Sun, your Son, was handed over to torture, and death, to the cross and the tomb—then you withdrew, tearful and dolorous, pierced by the bitterest sorrow of desolation.

And just as the sunflower pleases with its beauteous, golden coloration, so your virtue and humility pleased God himself, the Sun whom you adore. Out of the freshness of your fragrance, the hosts of angels and the choirs of virgins exult, and the Son of God, the Sun of justice, is enraptured with love most fervent!

PRAYER

O Maiden most fair, noble in humility, fragrant in virtue and radiant with pure charity! You delight the devout heart with a wonderful sweetness, you cleanse the mind of sins and impurities. You illuminate the soul with serenity and grace. May my soul melt and my heart be inflamed with passionate love for you! May your praise never cease from my lips, nor your love from my heart, nor your holy name from my memory so that I may always sense you to be with me as my protectress in temptation, my helper in perils, and my consoler in tribulation.

May you be my light when the sky grows gray and cloudy, my sweetness when the cup of life proves bitter, my liberator in adversity, the kind friend of my heart, and my faithful leader to the joy of the angels! Amen.

CHAPTER 22

THE PRECIOUS GOLD-GREEN JADE

in the Twenty-First Place in the
Crown of the Virgin

*"A Hebrew woman cast confusion into the house of
Nebuchadnezzar."*

Judith 14:16

This "Hebrew woman" prophetically mentioned in
the Book of Judith is certainly the Virgin Mary.[24]
For she is adorned with the splendid jewellery of virtues. From her lineage from the patriarch Abraham, she

---

[24]   The identification of the "Hebrew woman" in the Vulgate
text of Judith 14:16 as an allegorical figure of the Virgin
Mary reflects Medieval exegetical practice and would not be
the interpretation favored by most modern commentators.

is justly described as a "Hebrew." She is the springtide branch springing forth from the root of Jesse, which bore the most beautiful of all flowers—our Lord Jesus Christ—whose fragrance raises the dead to life, whose scent fills both the heavens and the underworld, and whose perfume delights and renews all humanity!

*   *   *

You, O Mary, are indeed this graceful branch, springing forth with celestial freshness and aromatic with charity and sanctity. But you proved also to be a rod of domination and confusion in the house of Nebuchadnezzar—that is, the devil. For you snapped the sceptre of his dark tyranny and tore apart the cruel yoke of the slavery of sin. And thus all generations rightly declare you to be blessed. Through you, salvation was given to the world, joy to heaven, honor and glory to God, peace to sinners, light to the blind, graces and blessing to the Church, and perpetual beatitude to the souls of the saints. Therefore, because you—after God himself—are the cause of all our joys, I extol you with a five-fold greeting, thus:

HAIL!

O, Queen of mercy, Bride of Christ, Mother of God, Daughter of the Father, Beloved of the Spirit, Light of the Church, Sweetness of love!

HAIL!

O, Queen of virgins, Empress of angels, Exultation of the good, Friend of peace, Virgin Mother, Most exquisite of women, Light of justice, Model of sanctity!

HAIL!

O, Beautiful rose, Tree of Life, Lily of Paradise, Resting place of the Trinity, Palace of the eternal Word, Happy door of Heaven, Comfort in distress!

HAIL!

O, One filled with grace, Mother of the poor, Advocate of sinners, Sceptre of justice, Joy of the soul, Peace of the sinner, Exultation of the heart!

HAIL!

O, Strength of our Faith, Firmament of the weak, splendor in darkness, Gate of mercy, Way of repentance, Fountain of sweetness, Cause of our salvation!

But because I yearn to honor you yet more, I humbly offer to you a precious stone of rarest gold-green jade, which I will carefully position in the twenty-first place in your noble crown. This polished stone sparkles with the brilliance of gold and glows with the greenness of spring—just as you, O Virgin, radiate the lustre of Divine wisdom and glow with the viridescence of holy deeds. In the shade of gold is the grace of wisdom signified; while the shade of green represents the purity of virginity.

Because, O Mary, you were the first to dedicate yourself to virginity for the glory of God, the Most High rewarded you with insight into the deepest mysteries of his holy wisdom. You fashioned a dwelling place, not merely for yourself, but for God himself! The eternal King chose you as the ivory palace in which to erect the throne of his glory.

And because it would be unbefitting for such a noble dwelling place to be without suitable adornment, he poured out upon you the seven gifts of the Holy Spirit, like seven priceless gems. Firstly, he gave you the gift of *Wisdom*, that you might be elevated into the ecstasy of celestial contemplation. Secondly, he adorned you with *Intelligence*, by which you were able fully to understand the depth of the divine mysteries. Thirdly, you were enriched with the gift of *Counsel,* that you would be prudent beyond all others. Fourth, God granted you *Knowledge,* that you might perceive all things with absolute clarity. Fifthly, he gave you the gift of *Fortitude,* that you should be strong and unwavering in the face of all adversity. Sixthly, you were endowed with *Piety,* that you may be a flowing river of mercy, overflowing with kindly charity. Seventhly, God granted you the grace of holy *Fear,* in order that you may be pure in mind and humbly reverent in the presence of his Divine Majesty.

PRAYER

I therefore beg you, most merciful Lady, that your grace may protect me. May it enlighten my senses, make chaste my body, sanctify my soul and inflame my heart.

May your strength enter into my being, illuminate my conscience and purify my flesh.

May your wisdom and virtue guard me against temptation, console me in tribulation and protect me from sin.

May your grace be with me, whether I am praying, meditating, reading, speaking, awake or sleeping.

May your mercy be with me in the hour of death, repelling the enemy who would seize my poor soul and drag it away to the inferno.

At that time, I pray that you will lead me—O sweet Mother—to the eternal joys of paradise! Amen.

CHAPTER 23

THE STAR ORION,

Mounted in the Twenty-Second Place in the
Crown of the Virgin

"I see one beautiful as a dove; she is surrounded by roses of spring, and the lilies of the valley." Thus speaks the Holy Spirit to you, O Mary, in words which express the wonder of God himself at your matchless beauty. You are indeed beautiful in faith, perfect in form, and lovely in sanctity: and truly as pure and innocent as the gentle dove.

Shining, starry constellations of angels and apostles surround you—together with fragrant roses of martyrs, aromatic violets of saints, and radiant lilies of holy virgins. For you exceed them all in innocence, wisdom, fortitude, and purity.

Which angel was ever more radiant than you?

Or what martyr ever showed more fortitude in sharing the sufferings of Christ?

Or what virgin saint ever rivalled you in immaculate chastity of body, mind, and soul?

I therefore present you with the star Orion, that it be placed in the twenty-second place in your holy diadem. This star is of outstanding brilliance, and its appearance foreshadows the arrival of renewing rains. Similarly you, O Mary, are stunningly splendid! Great was your splendor when you conceived God in your womb, yet greater still when you bore him to the world without loss of virginity. But greatest of all did this golden radiance become when you were exalted above the choirs of angels and archangels and crowned as Queen of heaven!

And, like Orion, your appearance brings with it gentle and welcome rain—the refreshing rain of grace and devotion, the nourishing rain of repentance and contrition, the transforming rain of compunction and tears, the delightful rain of sweetness and consolation.

PRAYER

O, most noble and kindly Mother of the incarnate Word of the eternal Father, you saved a lost world through the salvific fruit of your womb. You brought forth from your immaculate flesh through the heavenly dewfall of the Holy Spirit! O, illustrious Maiden, and Mother of the Highest King! O glorious Queen, adorned with all virtues and miraculously fashioned as the masterwork of the Creator!

I—an unworthy sinner, and thoroughly polluted with all vices, vagrant in heart, and fluctuating in mind—nevertheless desire to extol your majesty with praises, to celebrate your holy merits with song, to glorify your graces through devout prayers. But before I may do so, I beg you to heal my langors and infirmities, to inspire my senses with your light, to pour out your wonderful anointing into my heart—so that I may bring forth for you words inflamed with love and sanctified by grace.

> Lady Mary, maid Divine,
> Every holy virtue's shrine!
> In thy stance is noble grace;
> Beauty shines forth from thy face.
>
> Clemency in thy hands lies,
> Modesty shows in thine eyes.
> On thy lips is golden speech,
> Eloquence beyond all reach.

In thy soul is sanctity,
In thy mind, God's mysteries,
In thy heart, the flame of love,
In thy womb, the Lord above!

Be to us a shining light,
Guide us through life's little night;
Help us through this sea of sorrow,
Lead us to a blest tomorrow.

THE GEMSTONE BERYL,

in the Twenty-Third Place in the
Crown of the Virgin

"Thou hast fashioned a candelabrum of purest gold!"

Exodus 25:31

Most glorious Lady, you yourself are this candelabrum, in which God placed the light of his wisdom in order that he might search out and find the lost drachma.[25] The daughters of Jerusalem gaze upon you intently, that they may pursue the scent of your fragrance and run in the light of your virtue. You are an ark in which was placed the glorious treasures of divine

---

[25]   This is a reference to the parable of the lost coin in Luke 15:8-10.

motherhood. You are a golden thurible[26] from which devout prayer arises like incense before God. You are a gem-encrusted tabernacle, in which the Lord himself was physically enclosed!

You are indeed the Star of the Sea—to whom sinners sigh in supplication and angels bow in adoration. As two fiery cherubim, the archangel Gabriel and St. John the Evangelist both rejoice before your throne, singing songs of jubilant praise. From the thurible of purest gold—that is, from your most loving and immaculate heart—the rich aroma of incense, carrying with it the prayers of all the faithful, ascends into the very presence of God as an evening sacrifice of praise. Thus you are our perfect mediatrix and advocate before the Most High. You communicate to him our sincere devotion, while bearing to us the blessing of his mercy and pardon.

So it is that I—hoping you will intercede for me with your Son, the eternal Judge—present to you a precious beryl gemstone, well suited for the twenty-third place in your noble crown. This rare stone is bright and clear, transparent and flawless, possessing the wonderful

---

26   A thurible is a vessel in which incense is burned. See Revelation 8:3.

property of making those who possess or wear it invincible to their foes.

This stone may fittingly be compared to you, O Mary. For, by virtue of divine wisdom, you radiate a surpassing clarity and peerless luminance. Free of every stain of sin and immaculate from your very conception, you are perfectly clear and flawless. Thus it is that, as a transparent gem through which light passes without obstruction, the divine glory shines through you unimpaired and is made visible to eyes of the mortal heart. Conversely, as the unique mediatrix and privileged intercessor for humanity, you transmit our pleas, our cries, our tears and prayers to God, filtered and purified through your own unique goodness and mercy.

The ones who trust in you, you render invincible against the temptations of sin, the powers of demons and the perils of this life—for just as you yourself trampled the power of hell underfoot, so those assisted by your wonderful virtue shall never fall and those calling upon your holy name shall never be lost!

Chapter 25

THE DAISY FLOWER,

in the Twenty-Fourth and Final Place in the Crown of the Virgin

"King Solomon created a great throne of ebony, and coated it with shining gold. And, lo, this throne was adorned with six wings."

1 Kings 10:18

Our true Solomon—Christ, the King of Peace, unique in wisdom, and adorable in his glory—created for himself a most fitting throne, namely your womb, O Mary! In this, his ineffable Majesty was most pleased to rest.

You were indeed a throne of ebony. For there are three characteristics of ebony which are found in you in the highest degree. Firstly, it has a wondrous brilliance and polish. Secondly, it is by nature cool to the touch. Thirdly, it grows forth from the firm, elevated ground of the most lofty, mountainous regions of earth. And so you—O most glorious Virgin—shine with all the radiance of sanctity! Your heart remains unpolluted by the heat of passion or desire. And you sprang from the high and noble lineage of Abraham and the patriarchs, as a lovely princess descended from the royal house of David.

And the coating of gold with which Solomon adorned his throne corresponds with the divine wisdom and virtue with which God adorned you. Through this wisdom and virtue, you shine forth to all the world and illuminate the heavens themselves!

And the six wings affixed to the throne of Solomon correspond to the six maternal actions whereby you nourished and nurtured the infant Jesus. For you gave him food when he hungered; you nursed him with the milk of your bosom; you sheltered him in the bridal chamber of your womb. When he entered this world naked, you gently wrapped him in swaddling clothes. When he felt the fragilities of human infancy, you warmly embraced him in your motherly arms. And when he, of his own free will, had entered into the dark prison of our mortal state, you encouraged and guided him with a love untold—with the highest love of all.

Of all the works created by God, you are his true masterpiece, his *magnum opus,* who alone was worthy to carry and contain him, in both his flawless humanity and perfect divinity. In this, you transcend the entirety of Creation, the vast realms of space, the infinite constellations of stars, and the unseen legions of angels and archangels! Therefore—as my most noble Empress and my truest love—I have pledged to fashion for you a crown, not, indeed, as befits your splendor and glory, but as my poor abilities permit.

In the twenty-fourth and final place, I will now position a gentle daisy flower—humble, simple, and innocent, and yet unspeakably beautiful. The daisy is a flower with pure white petals, of round shape, delightful in its fragrance, and decorated with a centre of distinctive golden yellow. And you, Mary, display the pure white of those petals in your most immaculate soul, in the unstained serenity of your conscience, and in your virginal chastity. As a most beautiful queen, as a dove of the whiteness of snow, as a flawless lily, you are exalted to the heights of Zion, where you sing a song of glory and purity. This is a secret song of love, which no-one else can sing, and no mortal ear may hear, offered to the blessed name of the Lamb and of the eternal Father.

In your unbounded mercy, clemency, and justice—on account of which Christ drew you lovingly to himself—you may be compared to the perfect roundness of the daisy, without sharp edges and without irregularity. And your holy virtues exceed those of all others—even as a celestial fragrance, excelling all myrrh, incense, and perfume in its exquisite sweetness.

Finally, in your immaculate heart, radiant gold shines forth, like the centre of the daisy flower. For in your wisdom, you are brighter than the sun, and in your prudence, more luminous than the glowing moon, and in your grace, you transcend all the stars of the firmament. Through you indeed, the Son of God came forth to the world, the incarnate Deity, illuminating this earthly sphere, saving sinners, making the heavens to shine with a new and more sublime refulgence—and joining mortals and angels, Divinity and humanity, in an eternal and inviolable bond of holy Love!

CONCLUDING PRAYER

Please, accept, O holy Mary,
This, the crown I weave for thee—
Not of gold and gemstones earthly,
But of loving thoughts set free.

In it, I proclaim thy merits,
Striving to declare thy praise;
In it, to thy endless glory
Humble tribute do I raise.

Yet the awesome choirs of angels
And the stars which shine above
Dimly but reflect thy beauty,
Are but shadows of thy love.

For thy mercy I entreat thee,
Thy forgiveness I implore,
For thou art my hope, my sweetness,
Starry heaven's splendid door.

To thy Son, be endless honor,
Who is God and Lord supreme;
To thee be my love and longing,
To thee be each yearning dream.

Let me be dissolved in endless
Light, the realm of him and thee;
Pity thou this wretched sinner,
Pray to God, thy Son, for me!
Amen.